THE *Lure* OF SEA GLASS

OUR CONNECTION TO NATURE'S GEMS

By Richard LaMotte

Edited by Sally LaMotte Crane | Photographs by Celia Pearson

SEA GLASS PUBLISHING, L.L.C.

COPYRIGHT © 2015 BY RICHARD H. LAMOTTE

PHOTOGRAPHS © 2015 CELIA PEARSON

FIRST PRINTING 2015

 Published by Sea Glass Publishing, L.L.C.

P.O. Box 156 – Bishopville, Maryland 21813 U.S.A.

The Lure of Sea Glass – Our Connection to Nature's Gems

Printed in China

Design by 8 Dot Graphics

Library of Congress Control Number 2015900063

ISBN 978-0-9895800 1 4

Note: This compilation represents opinions of the author, his consultants, and editors. Every effort has been made to validate dates and events, however conflicting information was at times discovered. References to dates when bottles and glassware were manufactured represent periods of primary production or use. This book is intended solely to provide helpful direction for those interested in the collection and identification of sea glass.

www.seaglasspublishing.com

DEDICATION

To my wife Nancy, who has patiently assembled
and organized so many of the pieces of this puzzle
during its 10 years in the making.
I can only marvel at all that she manages
while raising two wonderful children,
creating sea-glass jewelry,
and running a small publishing business.

TABLE OF CONTENTS

FOREWORD

BY NANCY S. LAMOTTE

As I sit in my office I find myself wondering what time low tide might be. Like so many others, I would rather be on a beach looking for sea glass than doing anything else. It was this love of combing Chesapeake Bay beaches near our home that prompted me, some 15 years ago, to revive my skills and create a line of sea glass jewelry. Soon my husband, Richard, and children joined me in making sea glass hunting a family passion.

What is the lure of sea glass? To me, it's a nagging feeling that convinces me there is a precious jewel sitting in the sand at the water's edge, waiting for me to find it. If I don't get to the beach in time, it will be washed back out to sea or possibly picked up by someone else. But more importantly, it is also being out in nature with sun, salt air, and toes in the sand while water gently laps or crashes in waves at my feet. As the late naturalist John Muir wrote, "I only went out for a walk and finally concluded to stay out till sundown, for going out, I found, was really going in."

When I find a perfect piece of sea glass lying on the tide line, it is almost a spiritual experience. I feel as if I am receiving a message that life is good and everything will be alright.

Finding a piece of pure sea glass can feel like finding buried treasure. We don't pay for the experience or the treasure itself, so does that make it more valuable to us? Is the attraction to these unique shards simply that each piece is so completely different from any other, like a snowflake, but with an unknown history? With sea glass we can hold onto its past, tuck it in our pockets, and later pass our collection down to future generations.

In this continuously developing world we live in, there are few remaining public beaches where sea glass is abundant. It is human nature for us to want to discover the more secretive hideaways of these lovely charms.

In the following pages, you will continue on a journey with Richard LaMotte, author of Pure Sea Glass, to uncover more information about these wonderful gems we have grown to love. This time Richard touches on less technical and more emotional aspects of our special shards. Travel around the country and observe some prized finds from our nation's collectors. Learn why we unearth them and ponder their prior secret identities. After years of viewing thousands of private collections, Richard shares his knowledge by highlighting unique and rarely found pieces of sea glass so you can discover the identity of your more mysterious treasures.

I hope that you enjoy this journey as much as we have. Happy hunting!

"MY SOUL IS FULL
OF LONGING
FOR THE SECRETS
OF THE SEA,
AND THE HEART
OF THE GREAT
OCEAN SENDS A
THRILLING PULSE
THROUGH ME."

—HENRY WADSWORTH LONGFELLOW

THE LURE

Not long after the release of *Pure Sea Glass* in 2004, I was repeatedly asked by non-collectors, "Why are so many people drawn to sea glass?" My immediate response was to remark upon the collector's attraction to the colorful gem-like appearance of sea glass, the thrill of the hunt for a rare color, and the challenge to identify the source of a piece of history.

Of course, the sea, itself, lures us, its musical rhythms offering shifting moods of deep peace, wonder, or awe. Treading the shoreline, we are in tune with the elements—tides, waves, sun, moon, and stars. Some seek great solitude and others seek companionship, even if only with seals, porpoises, pelicans, and gulls. The meditative nature of combing the shore softens human tension and emotions, much like the patina on well-worn shards.

Still, searching deeper into the lure of sea glass, I found several surprises while meeting many new sea-glass collectors. The most memorable were the stories of extraordinary healing shared by individuals who held their stories quite privately; the coincidences of their discoveries seemed difficult for them to explain to others. Many had visited the shore looking for some solace or guidance and ultimately found an unexpected peace in the course of their sea-glass hunt. No monetary value could ever be placed on their cherished sea-glass finds; they are unmistakably priceless to the sole individual who went searching and found exactly what was needed at the time.

Amazed and curious, I was unprepared to press for further details right then. It seemed rude to request their names or ask to photograph their shards. How would I share with readers the deep emotional connection another person has to what one may view as merely a piece of broken glass? However, after hearing so many stories with a common theme, it became evident that I should try to record them.

Fortunately, we were able to locate a number of the collectors who earlier shared their personal triumphs, and they were kind enough to loan their sea glass for this book. I've done my best to recount the stories presented without any embellishment. For those who find any of these hard to believe, keep looking, and one day all of this will make sense to you. More than one collector has said, "I am not so sure I found it, but rather it found me."

Then, I realized that I also had a similar experience. Almost a month after the infamous day America was attacked in 2001, I was sitting in my car next to the Chesapeake Bay wondering if a sufficient breeze was building to windsurf to my favorite sea glass spot. Waiting for a sign, a voice interrupted the music on the radio for a special announcement from the White House. It was President Bush announcing he just ordered military strikes on terrorist camps inside Afghanistan. A new war had begun; he asked for patience and said it would be a long road. The date was October 7, 2001. I recall wondering if my wife was listening—thinking I should probably leave. Suddenly, a strong wind gust shook the car, and solid white caps began rolling in to shore. A clear sign I needed to stay and sail. The news remained on my mind as I wondered where this new war would take us. A quick sail to the beach, then after storing the rig, years of searching ended. Only three steps into my walk I found my first piece of elusive red sea glass, and it was perfect. By then, we had collected nearly well over 10,000 pieces of sea glass, but this was our first red one. Strapping it deep inside my sailing glove, I completed a hasty search for a few less exciting pieces and sailed back. My wife had just arrived to do some sea-glass collecting. I gave her the good news, the other news would wait. Like other collectors, I had a special shard, a date, a location, and a memory.

In addition to several inspirational stories, one can only explain the true "Lure" of sea glass by touching on its beauty, history, and mysteries. Portions of this book will explore identification of rare shards, as well as regional collections from around the United States. The reader is also treated to exquisite sea-glass images by Celia Pearson, a renowned museum and gallery artist. Over the past decade, Celia has established a reputation for capturing sea-glass in a manner that transforms a once simple collectible into an extraordinary art form.

Her detailed work is shown here in this image of what my wife considers her favorite find. After 16 years of collecting, this "honey bear" head was found near Smith Island, in the lower portion of Maryland's Chesapeake Bay. The mystery of its origin continues; similar objects were used on the lid of butter dishes and honey jars, but a search for the identical source is ongoing. Oddly enough, one of our tour guides, Trish Richards, had found a nearly identical piece years earlier. My wife and I were enamored by her contagiously cheerful spirit while combing the shores. Now Nancy and Trish share a bond that includes a common favorite treasure.

In 2004, at the time of writing these words in *Pure Sea Glass*, "There is a great healing power where water meets the shore," only half the picture was clear to me. As we age, we learn, and we begin to understand the greater picture of our life's surroundings—when to listen, when to follow, and when to lead. May this sequel volume, help lead you back to the shore.

HEALED TO PERFECTION

"WE MUST FREE
OURSELVES OF THE
HOPE THAT THE
SEA WILL EVER
REST. WE MUST
LEARN TO SAIL IN
HIGH WINDS."

— ARISTOTLE ONASSIS

Corolla Cure

An invitation to conduct the very first book signing for *Pure Sea Glass* came to me from Manteo Booksellers on the coastal Outer Banks of North Carolina. The event was scheduled for June 24, 2004, in a delightful historic bookstore nestled in a quaint village. Not long after setting up books and sea glass on a small card table, a couple walked in striding directly toward me. The woman wore a brilliant grin and a seasoned tan. She was holding my book rather securely, with both arms across her chest. Enthusiastically, she informed me how much she enjoyed the book, noting she had read it from cover to cover. Our first shipment had only landed on the Outer Banks two weeks earlier, so I was quite honored. Immediately after I signed her book, she asked if she could show me some of her favorite sea-glass shards. She presented a grouping of about eight well-worn shards in her hand, and one instantly stood out. I quickly pointed to a rare and stunning piece of red that sat on top and marveled, "I bet you remember when and where you found this little gem!" Her husband took a side step, looked at his wife, and said, "You really should share that story with him." She hesitated, her grin subsided a bit, and she took a deep breath. I was unsure what to expect next. Her story was rather enlightening.

"We live up in Corolla [North Carolina], but I'm from Ohio and had to rush back home for my brother's funeral when he died suddenly. I was devastated and miserable. When I got back to Corolla, I told my husband that I was going out to the beach and wasn't coming back until I found the best piece of sea glass I've ever found. Only a few minutes into my walk, I found this red piece, my first red piece ever, after many years of collecting."

She paused just long enough for her husband to chime in saying, "I saw her sprinting back over the dunes with something in her hand and must say, I have never seen anyone's attitude change so fast in all my life." She simply nodded, and when her cheerful smile returned, she looked down at her shard again. For me, it was not easy to find words to share in response, but I believe I told her to keep that in a safe place, since it's a very special prize. Years later, I saw her again, and she showed me photos of her collection carefully arranged in antique wooden typesetting drawers. This was the first of many stories of miracles by the shore.

"EACH DAY PROVIDES ITS OWN GIFTS." — MARCUS AURELIUS

Sea Glass FOR MARGARET

Hunched over
    like an egret,
my sister, Margaret,
    rummages barefoot
through a shoreline
    sharp with shells.

She can spot
    a speck of sea glass
and snatch it
    from the backwash
faster than you can say
    mea culpa.

Shards that aren't
    soft, Margaret
tosses back in the froth,
    keeps only the worn,
frosted scraps of light,
    finished

fragments
    with a jagged past
thrashed around
    so long they've been
sanded down,
    finally,

rounded off,
    smoothed over,
dull, but translucent
    and elusive.
My sister
    has spent

half a century
    of summers bent
on a handful
    of cobalt blue,
a riptide ruby
    or two.

BY JOHN SMITH

"REDS, YELLOWS AND ORANGES CONJURE UP SUNLIGHT AND FIRE, WHILE THE BLUES AND BLUE-GREENS EVOKE SNOW AND ICE, SEA, SKY AND MOONLIGHT."

— ANONYMOUS

A Fragile Heart

A new mother in Seattle, Washington, could only pray as she watched her three-day-old infant whisked away for heart surgery. The doctor was forced to use a microscope for a meticulous surgery on the 5-pound 10-ounce boy who was missing a critical ventricle in his three-chambered heart. They rerouted a main artery, and in the middle of the complex procedure, the mother and father were informed they should not expect him to survive. The collective efforts of frantic prayers appeared to be answered, and four weeks later, the family of three left the hospital together.

Nobody in the medical community expected Zeke to ever reach his second birthday, but somehow he kept beating the odds. He had another complicated surgery at age seven, and at 18, yet another risky open heart surgery, and days later, a pacemaker implanted. Seven years later, when in dire need of a heart transplant, they were told he was not a suitable candidate. Enumerable trips to hospitals were made during his 30 years. The doctors became as acquainted with their family, as they did their own staff; Zeke's rare condition was deeply studied and extensively shared. Finally, after a last-minute rally of energy a few days earlier to see a baseball game, Zeke declined. His mother lay beside him and saw him weaken as the defective heart stopped beating. She commented on her amazement at his positive attitude during his entire journey.

She shared this story as a gift to all who walk the shores of life. It took place during a walk with her husband not long after her son passed.

"The day we set out to walk to this particular beach, was one month to the day of his passing. I had been praying and praying for weeks that God would let me see him in Heaven. I wanted a vision, a dream, a sign—something—that would assure me that he is, indeed, in the arms of God. So we set out for the seven-mile hike to the shoreline, and my husband said, 'We need to find a red heart.' Ha ha! Eyes to the ground, we arrived at what was certainly the Glass Beach. Immediately my husband bent over and there it was, as though God had placed it on a pedestal with our names on it. One girlfriend of mine said, 'WOW – what more do we need to believe?'"

"LEAVE IT TO
MOTHER NATURE
TO IMPROVE
UPON SOMETHING
MANIPULATED
BY MAN AND
RETURNED TO HER
CARE AFTER IT
HAS SERVED OUR
TEMPORARY NEEDS."

— RICHARD LAMOTTE
FROM *PURE SEA GLASS*

Cobalt Blue

Milk of Magnesia

sharded by a winter storm

from shore-side garbage

to journey far,

tumbling and etching

into mermaids' tears

of misty cobalt blue.

I dance the

light fantastic

when you emerge

from weed cocoon

or shelly camouflage.

Argentium shall

enrobe you,

pearl and crystal be

your bridesmaids; and

you shall be

forever reunited

on a Viking knit

of harmony and love

and mystery.

BY BRYAN D. COOK
Ottawa, January 2013

First Peace

A special summer event was held at a seaside gallery in Lewes, Delaware, featuring our *Pure Sea Glass* book, framed sea-glass photography prints by Celia Pearson, and jewelry by my wife. Patiently waiting in line, a pair of women approached, and one quietly said to the other, "OK, go ahead and tell him." Unsure what to expect, I asked if she was a sea-glass collector. She reluctantly admitted, not really, but said she might now get into it after finding her first piece of sea glass.

"Almost a year ago, my mother was in her last days, and I was with her just before she passed. I was next to her in the hospital as she was drifting in and out.

Her last words to me were, 'Dearie, can you get me a Pepsi?' She passed away a moment later. About a week after all the family had left and gone home, I went out for a walk on the beach to clear my head. I recall stopping and specifically asking, 'Mom, please give me some sign that you are alright.' I looked down and directly next to my foot was this!"

She held out her hand and proudly showed me a frosted shard with an unmistakable Pepsi logo embossed on it. She then mentioned that she never had been a sea-glass collector before, but this made her understand why people collect it.

"THOSE WHO ARE FREE OF RESENTFUL THOUGHTS SURELY FIND PEACE."

— BUDDHA

"ALL THE RIVERS
RUN INTO THE SEA;
YET THE SEA
IS NOT FULL."

— KING SOLOMON

A Day of Loss

On the September day America was attacked in 2001, my wife and I were scheduled to fly at 8:05 that morning. Fortunately, we had already switched to an afternoon flight a few weeks earlier. We got off easily, with merely a cancelled flight, while others were not so lucky. That day did provide inspiration to not allow opportunities in life to pass us by, so when others urged me to write a book on sea glass, we agreed to take a risk. Not long after the book was released, I was contacted by a woman in Rehoboth Beach, Delaware, about a writers' conference. She was planning an event to raise funds to fight mitochondrial disease in honor of her nephew, who was suffering from the illness, and she asked to use the name of our book in the conference title— Writers at the Beach: Pure Sea Glass. We agreed, and during its successful seven-year run, I was introduced to many talented and inspirational individuals. One particular visitor was a sea-glass collector, and her story really stood out. At an event dinner, she shared with me her September 11th experience.

Working at her desk in the South Tower on Wall Street, she suddenly felt the building shake. Her boss told her to put on her government-issued Alcohol, Tobacco and Firearms (ATF) jacket and follow him down the stairs. At first she asked him why and didn't want to go, but he raised his voice and insisted—move now. While heading down over 70 flights of stairs, she distinctly recalled a sickening feeling about something she left behind. Oddly enough, she began thinking about her sea-glass collection. It was kept in a jar on her desk, and she worried that whatever evil was playing out may prevent her from seeing it again. On the way down, they felt another strong shake and picked up the pace down the stairs. When they got to the bottom, they heard strange noises, bangs from what she suspected was debris falling from above. The boss informed her they were heading to a secure bunker under Wall Street after a brief dash outside. Once there, she recalled her boss being approached by Mayor Giuliani, who seemed eager for details. He asked them what they had seen. She told him that when she looked up, there was smoke coming from both buildings, and unfortunately, we saw some "jumpers." It was heartbreaking to see. She did not mention to him one very unforgettable image. She added, "I recall seeing a woman who had jumped, her dress was lifting up over her face, and she was desperately trying to keep it down. What struck me was how she was trying to protect her dignity, even in the last seconds of her life."

"I NEVER MET
A COLOR
I DIDN'T LIKE."

— DALE CHIHULY

"THERE IS SPLENDID
IRONY IN COLLECTING
SEA GLASS, SINCE THIS
ALLURING TROPHY
SOUGHT AFTER IN
THE SHIFTING SAND
WAS ONCE MERELY
SAND ITSELF."

— RICHARD LAMOTTE
FROM *PURE SEA GLASS*

Two Blue

A woman residing near Washington, D.C., asserts that her heart will always remain at the Jersey Shore where she grew up. She constantly marveled at the treasures she picked up along the ocean's edge. Until recently, she would donate her sea-glass finds to the collections of others, but now a small hurricane jar sits proudly on a coffee table holding a colorful bounty.

She explained that four years ago, she was struggling with a deeply personal issue, and her feelings were very conflicted. During her summer vacation at the Jersey shore, she awoke very early one morning, specifically to spend some time alone walking on the beach. It was August, and as the new sun rose, everything was sparkling. She shared, "I find great peace in walking, and though I am not a very religious person, I often find myself talking to God and asking for guidance."

On this particular day, while walking and weighing options about her future, she realized something unusual was happening. It seemed that every few steps, she was finding a piece of sea glass. Not just white, green, and amber but varying shades of soft blue and sea-foam green. After pausing to stare at the wonderful little gems, she realized she was still torn over her big decision. Suddenly, she had the peaceful feeling that it was all somehow connected.

While she had collected sea glass for years, she had never found any cobalt blue or red pieces before that day.

Looking skyward, she said, "OK God, I know you have a plan for me, but I don't know which way to go. If you believe it would be a mistake to go down a new road I'm considering, give me a sign. If I find a blue or red piece of sea glass, I'll have my answer." She immediately thought making this demand was foolish and felt rather guilty, so laughed at her comment and continued walking.

"I don't remember if it was two steps or 10, but right there in front of me was the most beautiful piece of cobalt-blue sea glass I'd ever seen. I was stunned to say the least; I started laughing as I looked up to ask, are you sure about this? Meanwhile, I had little doubt about the message. Then in my next step, there in front of me was a second cobalt-blue piece. It was smaller than the first, but of no less of a sign, perhaps reinforcement just in case I had any doubt."

Holding tightly to the pieces she found that morning, she ran back to the house. She also knew her struggle was over, and her decision was made. "Four years later, I have never looked back with regret."

PENIKESE ISLAND: *At the mouth of Buzzards Bay, in southeastern Massachusetts, sits a tiny 75-acre island named Penikese. It is about 12 miles southwest of Cape Cod and just north of charming Cuttyhunk Island.*

In 1905, the state of Massachusetts established a leper hospital on the island, and over a period of 16 years, obligated 36 men and women to reside there. Many left behind families and life as they once knew it, not knowing if they would ever be released. By 1921, 14 of the patients were buried on the island, and 13 remaining patients were transported on a hospital train to a federal facility down in Carville, Louisiana. Only a few were ever released.

In 2010, Massachusetts poet Eve Rifkah captured the essence of life on the island after an intensive study. In her work titled Outcasts: The Penikese Island Leper Hospital, Rifkah chronicled the lives of numerous inhabitants. One named Julia is a 60-year-old sea-glass collector whose cherished finds help provide her hope in the poem "Sea Glass."

Sea Glass

pale green glimmer caught in seaweed
hazed by ocean rake
back and forth   scrape sand and shell
held to light   shadowed edge of letters
L A S
another find for Julia's treasures
she keeps in a tin next to her bed

cobalt bits her favorites   she calls them sapphire
glass from milk of magnesia bottles
and greens so many greens
pastels of canning jars   emerald mentholatum jars
one tiny sun of yellow   a mystery

sometimes shards of crockery
a bit of castle, black capped bird

girl in a ruffled cap, a willow sprig

at Christmas, Mrs. Parker gives her a white platter
and a thin layer of wool batting
to arrange her gems—greens
next to blues   frosted whites   chips reveal
centers like jellies
        forever empty
        forever full

here the pieces come to rest
she imagines other lives
imagines being whole

BY EVE RIFKAH from the book
"Outcasts: The Penikese Leper Hospital 1905-1921"
Published by Little Pear Press, 2010.

"SIT IN REVERIE
AND WATCH THE
CHANGING COLOR
OF THE WAVES
THAT BREAK
UPON THE IDLE
SEASHORE OF
THE MIND."

— HENRY WADSWORTH LONGFELLOW

Giving Thanks

In March of 2006, I was dragging luggage through a busy Los Angeles International Airport in preparation for a flight home. Agents selected my luggage, along with that of another young woman nearby, and walked us over to have it scanned by a massive machine. During the awkward wait, I asked if she was heading home and soon found that she was not only on the same flight but also was a customer of my day job. She mentioned her home was Lavallette, New Jersey, a town that I knew was on the Jersey Shore.

A while later, I found myself seated near her in the terminal. What happened next was rather unusual, since I almost never strike up conversations with strangers at airports. Knowing she lived at the beach, something kept nudging me. So finally I asked if anyone in her family had ever collected sea glass. She actually said yes, quietly adding her mother was a big collector, and so was her grandmother. In their house, there was a large bowl with an heirloom collection of sea glass bequeathed by her grandmother that the family added to on a regular basis. This day happened to be one of the very rare occasions I had traveled with a copy of *Pure Sea Glass*, so I pulled it out and asked if she would like to take it home to her mother. After she had some time to peruse it, I offered to sign

it for her mom. She seemed content with the gesture, and after I signed it, she said she had a story to share. The following story came as quite a surprise, given that I was sitting in a busy airport with someone I'd just met, but soon I understood why I was being nudged to lighten my luggage by one book.

"My mother works at a bank, and one day, this rather large man was waiting in line for the teller. She could clearly tell he was distressed about something. She waved him over to her desk and offered to help him. He admitted that he was a bit distraught, since he had just come from the doctor's office where he was told that unless he started some form of regular exercise right away, he was very likely to have a heart attack. So my mother told him he just needed to walk the beach daily, and she proceeded to draw out a map showing him her favorite spots to find sea glass. She explained to him what to look for and told him to come back soon and show her his finds. After making a few trips to collect sea glass, he not only returned with glass shards, but in time he managed to lose weight and get healthier. She eventually found out he had no family, so she invited him for Thanksgiving dinner. He now comes every year and even visits for Christmas. It's like he's become part of the family."

"WITHOUT A FAMILY, MAN, ALONE IN THE WORLD, TREMBLES WITH THE COLD."
— ANDRE MAUROIS

"A DIAMOND IS
CREATED BY NATURE
AND ARDUOUSLY
REFINED BY MAN,
WHILE SEA GLASS IS
WHAT MAN CREATES
AND NATURE
REFINES FOR US."

— RICHARD LAMOTTE
FROM *PURE SEA GLASS*

Rebirth of Sea Glass

It is there you lie
 shimmering.....
   glistening.....
     waiting.....

Will you soon be overtaken by
     the ebb and flow of the sea?
Will you be buried in a myriad of pebbles
     waiting to be free?
Or will you be lifted up ever so gently
     by an admiring soul......by me?

I reach down to lift you up into
     the palm of my hand
And carefully brush away
     the few grains of sand.

          WONDERING.....

Where have you been? What story could unfold?
Your smoothness lends clues of an epic untold.
Gingerly I place you in the warm confines of my pocket.

          WONDERING.....

Where will this new journey take you?
Be it near.....
               or afar.....

Wherever the journey takes you
You will continue to be
 shimmering.....
   glistening.....
     and waiting.....for many more to admire.

It is your new beginning
     Now you are..........reborn.

BY MARABETH GROGAN
©2009 Simply from the Sea

Shard Inheritance

Writer Stephen Fried made plans to visit our home in the course of writing an article for Parade Magazine on collecting sea glass. He was enthusiastic about heading out onto the Chesapeake Bay in kayaks to investigate our favorite spot for finding glass shards. He swiftly began picking up every piece in sight before realizing I was being a bit more selective, leaving the whites, greens, and browns for those with smaller collections than ours. If there is one thing an experienced collector enjoys, it is seeing the excitement of others on a good day. I learned that Stephen was a writing professor at Columbia University and a best-selling author. Prior to our hunt, he had only shared a limited background on the family's passion for sea glass. In the end, he wrote an exceptional article for Parade. One never knows what the next tide might bring in.

Later, Stephen shared some more details of his father's passion for sea glass and how his family kept that going. I asked him to contribute to this book, and he truly captured the essence of the lure of sea glass.

JERRY FRIED'S SHARD INHERITANCE

I don't know when my dad first started looking for sea glass because, frankly, I didn't get it. To me, bending over for glass just interrupted the long walks and long talks that were my family's primary form of in-depth communication during our summers on Long Beach Island, New Jersey. We saved up "topics" for those walks for months, because the rest of the year, when we were together, nobody could get a word in edgewise.

But as my dad, Jerry Fried, got older and started spending entire summers at the shore, and my mom went out on the beach with him less, I guess he had more private walking time. And after a while, he had a pretty substantial collection of well-cooked sea glass... which I pretty much ignored.

Then he died at the age of 62, in the winter of 1997. And several weeks later, I did something he would have appreciated. I asked my mother and my two brothers and my wife's parents and her two sisters (and all the various spouses, significant others, and the first four grandchildren) to come to the family shore house together for a week around the 4th of July. It was going to be a new tradition whether anyone liked it or not. At the time, 17 people in six small bedrooms, two full and two half-baths, and an outdoor shower.

So, it provided a lot of incentive for beach walking. And, much to my surprise, I found myself joining the family beach business and looking for sea glass, as did my younger brothers, Jeff and Dan. And we instructed the youngsters how to do it, as if it had always been a multigenerational family tradition—which it suddenly was. Initially, the kids—Emma, Anna, Jake, Eli and Miranda—only wanted to find glass washed up on shore; they were nervous about standing knee-deep with their backs to the ocean, watching for shards momentarily exposed by the receding waves. But, eventually, they figured it out. Soon, it was not uncommon to see a gaggle of us combing the beaches of southern Long Beach Island,

heads bent down like sandpipers looking for food, with passersby wondering why every few minutes someone yelled out "green!" or "brown!" or "clear!" or, if they were lucky, "blue!" And since, for my brothers and me, this was all so tied to our father, when we found something great, we would often mutter under our breaths "thanks, Dad," as if he had dropped the shard there.

We began family glassing traditions. I started buying everyone a little glass container every year so they could keep the season's "catch" separate. We developed our own glassing language. (We were "glassheads" and the people who competed with us by searching with nets and sieves rather than bending down and getting their hands sandy were "glassholes.") And to keep everyone engaged, we created a family contest—on the last night of the weeklong beachfest, after the glorious grilled fish and before the ceremonial July 4th flag cake my mom loved to make, we had a glass-off. Everyone submitted their best shards to the competition, and we created enough categories that every kid could win something (and as more kids came, we added more categories.) Best green, best blue, best white, best shape, best piece with letters on it, best whatever we could think of, and then "best in show." The non-glassers in the family—my wife, Diane, my mom, Estelle, and my sister-in-law, Lori—were the judges. They had clipboards and everything.

The one category we never had was "best red" because, of course, nobody in our family had ever found one. A red had been my father's holy grail, and he passed that search on to us. Then one day, about 10 years into the family glassing obsession, we were all out wading in a late afternoon low tide when what appeared to be something reddish briefly glistened in the shallow water between my brother Dan and me. I was closest to it and got there first. When I held it up and hollered "RED!" my pre-teen nephew, Jake, stood yelling in the surf in disbelief for what seemed like forever. We have since found a couple more, but there's nothing like your first red.

Today, there is, unfortunately, a lot less glass at the Jersey Shore than there used to be, and the kids are in college, and they want to walk the beaches with their boyfriends and girlfriends. So I find myself glassing alone more than I used to, often getting up at 5:30 am to be the first to check out special spots before there are anyone else's footprints in the sand. When I find something noteworthy, I take a cellphone picture of it and text it to all my grown-up glassheads, wherever they are.

If I find something that seems truly amazing, I am lucky enough to have made friends with (and once got to glass with) the world's expert on shardism (and the author of this book), Richard LaMotte, who indulges my queries no matter what the hour, usually explaining—very kindly—that what I found isn't quite as amazing as I think it is. I have only really impressed him once. Early one morning, I found a very unusual shard of an old plate, with an image of two Dutch children kissing on it. I texted a picture to the family, and then to Richard, who thought it was amazing, asked if he could use a picture of it in a presentation and, now, if he could include it in this book.

I told him of course. And then I whispered to myself, "thanks, Dad."

"WHATEVER THE
REASON FOR
COLLECTING,
MOST SHARE THE
COMMON GOAL
OF FINDING A
NEW PIECE MORE
EXQUISITE THAN
THE LAST."

— RICHARD LAMOTTE
FROM *PURE SEA GLASS*

Piece of China

Searching for sea glass with a member of the family or a close friend frequently leads to a lifetime of fond memories. A woman from Connecticut shared that she had recently taken her five-year-old son to a beach on Long Island Sound and was attempting to teach him the joys of sea glass hunting. He had not had much luck but finally came running to his mother, proudly holding a white shard with some printing. Excitedly passing it over to her, the mother examined it and with great enthusiasm said, "Oh wow! You found a beautiful piece of China!" The boy's face suddenly looked worried and confused, then with a slow and almost tearful response he said, "Does that mean we have to send it back?"

"WE ARE TIED
TO THE OCEAN.
AND WHEN WE GO
BACK TO THE SEA,
WHETHER IT IS TO SAIL
OR TO WATCH -
WE ARE GOING BACK
FROM WHENCE
WE CAME."

— JOHN F. KENNEDY

Lost and Found

One summer afternoon in 2006, I was closing a lecture in a quaint bookstore named Bunch of Grapes on Martha's Vineyard in Massachusetts. After sharing some stories provided to me by collectors over the past two years, I asked if anyone had questions. A woman politely raised her hand and requested to share an important story of her own.

 "A few years ago, I was at a very low point in my life. For a long time, I had struggled financially to keep my house and garden, since they meant everything to me. Finally they were lost, and I had to leave my home. I was devastated. Soon afterward, a friend of mine who lived on the island of Nevis asked me to come for an extended visit while I tried to sort things out. On my first day there, my host left to get things at the market, so I decided to take a long walk on the beach. The beaches were pristine white sand, and there were no footprints, no shells, or sea glass anywhere. Walking along the edge of the water, a wave came up over my feet, and as it receded, I saw something land right next to my foot. I looked down and thought it was simply a piece of a shell. But then I picked it up and turned it over. It was not a shell but actually was a porcelain shard. I could hardly believe my eyes when I looked closely and saw what was clearly printed on the shard—a House and a Garden."

As she held the shard up for all to see, the people in attendance collectively gasped. I felt privileged to be on hand to share that extraordinary moment.

In 2014, I was able to connect with the collector, who still lives in Vineyard Haven. She explained that she is back on steady ground and still cherishes this shard. When I telephoned, she told me she quickly picked it up and was holding it in her hand. Later, she added that she is once again the proud owner of an actual house and garden.

Beachglass

I am a collector of beachglass

and have been one for many a season.

I can tell from a shard no larger

than my thumbnail—from the arc of its curve,

from its shape, weight, and thickness, even

from the angle of its breaking—its origin

on a bottle: base, body, neck, or rim.

And with each piece I find, I like to stop

and rest for a while, turning it over

carefully between thumb and forefinger,

noting its color, amber, green, or clear,

it's source, soda, beer, whisky, wine bottle,

and its size, nip, pint, fifth, quart, or magnum.

But the luster—it's all in the luster!

It's got to be frosted like gumdrops—

no shine or clarity—opaque.

And if it's not perfect—

if there's a shine or a glitter,

or if a rough edge catches my finger—

then I toss it back to the sea

as I would an undersized lobster

to be buffeted by waves and sand

and harvested in another season.

These bits of colored glass I find

are dear to me like rubies, diamonds,

emeralds, and semi-precious stones, and

I like to think what I would do with them.

I would make a necklace for a gypsy bride,

smith them into silver bracelets, and send them

to every woman I have ever loved,

or make a mosaic of unknown design

in thanks for every poem I've ever written

and offer it to the wind, the sea, and the sun.

This aimless path I walk between bits

of broken glass is the only thing I know—

the only thing I hold on to. I will

be back for another season's harvest.

BY RICHARD CAMBRIDGE

"THE LEAST
MOVEMENT IS OF
IMPORTANCE
TO ALL NATURE.
THE ENTIRE OCEAN
IS AFFECTED BY
A PEBBLE."

— BLAISE PASCAL

Symbols in the Sand

I n the shadow of Barnegat Light on the northern end of Long Beach Island, New Jersey, sits a quaint shop featuring charming art by local artists and its owner, Cricket Luker. Following a particularly busy event just 15 minutes south earlier that day, I arrived at the quiet north end not expecting a crowd. The gathering at Wildflowers by the Lighthouse provided the opportunity to spend more time with sea-glass collectors and my hosts. A staff member at the shop heard me share some stories from other collectors about their extraordinary experiences when finding a special shard. She waited for the visitors to leave and then began to tell me about a special pair of shards she kept at home. Both she and her avid sea-glass collecting friend were baffled, never having seen anything like them.

She had two sea-glass bottle bottoms at home, each with only one huge letter on the bottom. In the past, she had found plenty of shards with small lettering, logos, and numbers but nothing like these. When asked if they were clear glass and if the single letter was very broad and thick, she confirmed they were. I let her know they must be milk bottle bottoms, and the letter would signify a local dairy that supplied the milk. She had no knowledge of their origin, but clearly the shards meant a lot to her, and so she proceeded to tell me why these had a particularly special meaning.

"I'm not a religious person, spiritual, yes, but not religious. I didn't know what to make of these bottle bottoms when I found them. It was about 10 years ago, I had a very rough seven-month-stretch when my mother passed away and, a week later, my dog of 13 years, Molly, passed away. Then, finally, my father passed on my parents' anniversary.

Right after my dog died, I found this perfectly clear but frosted bottle bottom with a bold 'M' on it and silently asked my late mother if this was some type of sign. Then about 30 days after my father passed, I walked the beach, extremely upset about all the events that had happened. I literally thought I saw a jellyfish lying in the sand but found it was nearly an identical bottle bottom, but this time with a bold 'N' written on the bottom. My parents' names were Norcross and my father, Monty, had been a milkman when I was growing up. I had been asking for some sign that they were OK, and when I found these, all I could say was, 'Thanks – OK.' The strange thing was that these were found at times when almost no other sea glass was on the beach. Neither my friends, nor I, have ever found anything like them since."

"NATURE IS THE GLASS
REFLECTING GOD,
AS BY THE SEA
REFLECTED IS THE SUN,
TOO GLORIOUS
TO BE GAZED ON
IN HIS SPHERE."

— BRIGHAM YOUNG

Soul Searching

An avid collector and customer from Mattapoisett, Massachusetts, who had routinely sent photos of very unique items she had been finding not far from her home, wrote saying that today was a very special day.

"I WENT TO THE BEACH TODAY,
AND I FOUND JESUS."

"THE SEA, ONCE IT CASTS ITS SPELL, HOLDS ONE IN ITS NET OF WONDER FOREVER."

— JACQUES YVES COUSTEAU

Sea Glass FOR MIMI

At sea, cheap brassy-colored bottles get

tossed overboard: the fisherman's brown beer,

the matron's lemon-yellow sun tan oil,

the sea-sick youngster's bright green ginger ale,

the blue-haired widow's deep blue laxative.

They spiral down, return to sand, and break.

The jagged pieces roam the ocean floor,

are scrubbed and scoured, tumbled, tossed – in sun-

less rhythm at the moon's command – until

ground back to origins or offered up

on shore. Now purified by salt and buffed

by time, they glow among the shells and tide-

line scrap in subdued shapes and subtleties

of opal, topaz, jade and aquamarine.

BY DONALD WERNER

Look Toward the Surf

A disheartened father from northern Virginia wrote to share a collector's story following the death of his adult son in January of 2008. His hope was to gather information about a special piece of sea glass he found while walking the seashore in solitude, on a beach quite familiar to both men. He provided this story soon after visiting the Outer Banks of North Carolina in June of that same year:

"I lost my son, Dave, in January. He was killed in Iraq while serving our country. Coming to the beach this year was hard because we have come to the same place for 20 years, and here there are many memories of him as a little boy, a high school graduate, and a 26-year-old getting ready to go to Fort Benning.

I was walking north near Ocean Sands after lunch last Wednesday, well after the shell beds had been thoroughly picked over, and finally asked God for a sign that Dave was okay. I asked specifically for a piece of beach glass. Almost immediately, after I prayed that out loud, I was prompted to look toward the surf, away from the shell line. As soon as I did, I saw this piece of glass doing cartwheels, retreating to the ocean in a wave. I was able to grab it, and I knew I had something special as soon as it was in my hand.

We always bring a copy of your book with us to the beach and discerned that it was black glass.

Given the story behind it, and that it was a direct answer to my prayer, I'm just a little curious to know as much about it as possible."

He sent me the shard for review. It was a classic, a rare fragment from the lower wall (heel) of a Dutch or English "onion-style" wine bottle. It was obviously from a hand-blown vessel, the deep olive-colored piece of black glass revealed one large bubble and an abundance of other bubbles in its core. Specks of red from the iron oxide were leaching from the glass and adding color to its surface. Colonial black glass was made using iron slag—after 200 years at sea, it was releasing an iron precipitate.

All the features pointed to an estimated age of the early to mid-1700s. As I pointed out to Dave, "It very well could have been part of a shipwreck, and you possibly witnessed its first tumble on U.S. soil." What I never mentioned to him was something a bit more unusual. I grew up in Virginia and knew the geography of the state rather well. I noticed the shard looked like a large portion of the state, and that distinct large bubble in its surface was, in my opinion, located specifically on northern Virginia where his family home had always been.

Soon after sharing my basic assessment of his shard, Dave wrote back to point out that prior to finding the

shard on the beach, he happened to use a reference to sea glass in the eulogy for his son. Below is a segment of the eulogy that seemed to echo his hope for peace.

"HERE'S WHAT I KNOW

There are two things going on here. The first is the existential reality of death, and today more than any day so far in this sequence of events, I feel the cold embrace of that reality. Shakespeare called sleep 'the balm of hurt minds.' That's so very true, because each morning when I wake up and my mind starts operating, the very first thing I'm confronted with—my head still on the pillow and the sleep still in my eyes—is that existential reality that Dave is gone. I don't know when and if that ever changes. Maybe now it's like a piece of broken glass, tossed into the ocean, still shiny, jagged, and sharp. And as the years go by, the color will change, and the edges, sanded and salted with time, will have a smoothness that's manageable and soft to the touch. I don't know... but I do know that the opening act of every day of my life will have this reality as its prelude. It is what it is. What's done is done."

"I WIPED AWAY
THE WEEDS
AND FOAM,
I FETCHED
MY SEA-BORN
TREASURE
HOME."

—RALPH WALDO EMERSON

Sea Glass by Region

Along both coasts of the Continental United States, from the 42nd parallel north (covering roughly the top third of the nation), sea glass is often aggressively tumbled into smaller and more rounded shards than those found in central and southern coastal regions. Battered shards are also common along the southern shorelines of the Great Lakes, where beaches are exposed to strong northerly winds. Relentless waves rinse stone-laden beaches turning glass shards into small gems. The conditioning process is generously accelerated by robust wave action and winter ice on coarse and rocky shores. In stark contrast are the soft, welcoming coral sand beaches of Florida, which leave broken shards more in their original condition. Thus, a well-worn shard found in Florida has probably spent several more decades taking its shape than a similar shard found on a northern shore, the latter buffed smooth in maybe only 10 to 20 years.

The collections shown on the following pages represent a smattering of items from American sea-glass enthusiasts selected from the perimeter of our country. It was a great privilege to work with these individuals, and we deeply appreciate their cooperative spirit by sharing some of their finds for this book. Many provided samples of unique treasures, ones few of us will ever find in the days ahead as supplies of this great collectible continue to disappear.

Sea glass collection courtesy of Danielle Perreault – Coastal Southern Maine

Maine

The state of Maine very likely has the highest percentage of sea-glass collectors per capita in the world. Its nearly 3,500 miles of tidal coastline on the Atlantic seaboard is the largest total of any state. Maine has over 3,000 islands, many rich with history of settlers from Europe. In the late 1800s and early 1900s, hauling spent glass from the islands to dump inland was uncommon. So it is easy to understand why so many shards still show up in the nooks and crannies of their many rocky shores. The perpetual chilly waters and pebbly beaches make beachcombing far more inviting than swimming or sunbathing, even in summer. Thus, containers of sea glass are a frequent sight in Maine's family cottages. The vast majority of coastal Maine residents are rather familiar with sea glass even if they have never collected it themselves.

In Kennebunk, a pair of sisters who have collected sea glass most of their lives have begun an effort to establish a museum specifically for sea glass, along with a traveling exhibit. This photo is a testament to the considerable amount of tableware found on several of their protected Down East beaches. Other shorelines with more severe wave action would have created far smaller shards and left these more difficult to identify.

Just right of center is a rare piece in this collection, since it is quite challenging to find pieces of Carnival glass on the shore. The shard of Marigold Carnival glass displays the Hobstar pattern by Imperial Glass and is likely from a biscuit jar. The iridescent golden color remains only within its deeply embossed pattern. Below it is the top of a unique pressed-glass stopper for a cruet displaying a slight lavender tint from oxidized manganese, which places its manufacture date from 1880 to 1915. The golden yellow shard in the center appears to be part of a pressed-glass ashtray due to the squared-off corner and flattened edge on top. Above it is a vivid purple, pressed-glass fruit or punch bowl shard showing elements of the Princess pattern first designed in 1894. On the left are two tumbler bases, one peach and the other clear. On the far upper right, the lone bottle shard is an amber Owens-Illinois bottle bottom from a small sampler bottle. The "I" inside "O" logo, along with a stippling pattern, places it in the late 1950s to 1960s.

Massachusetts

Many years ago, Cape Cod in Massachusetts and its neighboring islands were good sources for sea glass. In recent decades, shards have become more difficult to find, and serious collectors have ventured north to Gloucester or west to Buzzards and Narragansett Bays. This collection comes from the western shores of Buzzards Bay, where miles of coastline still produce shards that reflect the region's rich history.

Many of the items shown here include apothecary and chemical-laboratory bottle stoppers. An assortment of "penny-head"-style stoppers, named for their upright coin-like shape, include the two light lavender ones in front, next to the amber stopper, and the teal and amber stoppers at top right. Another common apothecary form is the amber mushroom-style version on the left. The rare cobalt-blue stopper has a short, yet wide, inner post and was likely used to seal a laboratory or medical powder. Most of these classic pieces are circa late 1800s, even though some items, like the penny-head stopper-style, have continued long afterward.

In the center is the top of a large decanter stopper, its thick glass with a hollow center displays a slight lavender coloration from manganese and subtle facets down the side. Above it are two, nearly identical, large soft green and soft blue cap-stoppers for late 19th-century fruit/pickle jars. They measure about 2.2 inches across with an inner core post of 1.5 inches. The soft green one exhibits a clear "TW Co" logo, which means it was made by Thomas Wightman & Company of Pittsburgh between 1872 and 1893. Pittsburgh glass houses were famous for their fruit jars and window glass during the 1800s. One well-known enterprise started in 1883 was the Pittsburgh Plate Glass Company known as PPG today.

One striking and unusual find is the large green, "square-head" cap stopper in the center. This would have been used on a rather wide-mouth apothecary bottle that had a cork sheath around the collar of the bottle, rather than on the post of the stopper.

The white piece just to its right is the top portion of an ornate perfume stopper with feathery, petal-like extensions above the post. Among the various other clear stoppers are two rare orange beads and an orange cat's-eye marble.

Sea glass collection of Louise and Ben Rogers – Mattapoisett, Massachusetts

A sand-buffed bottle of Fitch's shampoo (upper right) was a common sight at barber shops in the early 1900s. Famous for his innovative dandruff shampoos, F.W. Fitch became known as the "Shampoo King." His heavily researched formulas were first designed to treat his own scalp issues, but his concoctions caught on. The pride of Des Moines, Iowa, during the 1920s through 1940s, the Fitch's brand became as famous in that era as Head and Shoulders today. The piece here shows screw-cap threads and mold lines reaching up to the lip, confirming its post-1900 age.

Many hair-tonic bottles at that time had narrow mouths with very small orifices to help limit the amount dispensed. A good example is the small white doughnut-shaped lip in the center. Attempts to create such a small opening prior to automated molding would have been a challenge.

Also in the center of this image is a lavender patent-medicine bottle neck, its color and lack of mold lines placing it prior to 1900. Below it, a long soft blue, patent-medicine-style bottle neck shows a hand tooled, pre-1900 lip shard. The blue one next to it appears to be only slightly more recent. The oldest object shown is likely the soft green, tapered lip of a bottle, at left, with specks of iron staining on its surface. The crude hand-tooled lip was possibly formed in the mid- to late 1800s. Within this collection are two domed kick-ups from the bottom of bottles circa 1900 and some small vials which could be for pharmaceutical use.

Long Island Sound, New York

Many bays along the East Coast are still rich with historic shards that provide solid clues to activities once popular in the region. Unlike aggressively worn shards found on rocky northern coastlines and buffed by relentless open sea waves, these from Long Island Sound seem to have had less torment. Some suggest origins from a local dump site while others hint of a nearby amusement park.

A mid-1800s porcelain doorknob with remains of a brown glaze is a rare find, as well as a peach-colored stopper. The blue Blob-top soda lip and neck in the lower right also dates to the mid- to late 1800s. Most of the others are turn-of-the-20th-century pieces, such as the NY initialed beer bottle shard.

Just below the doorknob is a wide-mouth stopper marked "ENOS" ringed by worn-off text that once read "PREPARED BY PATENT." Its shaft would have had a thin cork strip and would have been used to seal the Eno's Fruit Salt Derivative Compound for constipation relief. It arrived from London to be sold by agent Harold Ritchie & Company of Madison Avenue, New York, beginning in the 1880s. The soft green color is consistent with their earliest bottles. They used more aqua-colored bottles in the early 1900s when "ENOS" was removed from the center of the stopper. The product remains on the market today in England sold as "Eno" in plastic bottles.

The unique ceramic frog was a figural piece since its base was cleanly molded, never attached to a larger object such as a lid. Thus, one would suspect this was a toy to go along with the many marbles from the early 20th century. Figural items, such as this frog, are considered extremely rare by sea-glass collectors.

In the lower left, rust is leaking from wire within a piece of safety glass, popular in windows and doors of schools and government buildings during the 1950s. Also from that general era is the large pressed-glass pitcher handle seen at top and the wall of a pressed-glass vase below the frog. To the left of the frog is a familiar starburst pattern cut or molded into the bottom of a wine glass.

The brass ball bearing is very unusual and similar in size to musket shot or pistol shot but seems too refined for vintage ammunition.

Sea glass collection of HL Sea & Beach Glass Jewelry – Long Island Sound and Great Peconic Bay

Chesapeake Bay, Maryland
EASTERN SHORE

Both shores of the Chesapeake Bay, the world's largest estuary, have provided collectors with historic remnants for centuries. Paleontologists collect ancient shells and teeth from 50-foot Megalodon sharks that lurked in the sea 15-million years ago. More recent relics are from our colonial settlers who discarded black glass gin, rum, and wine bottles along the Chesapeake shorelines. This continued into the first half of the 20th century, as early plantation owners and farmers hauled refuse to the edge of their properties—out of sight. Erosion has extracted glass from some rubbish sites but rising water levels have begun to cover many of the beaches, making sea glass collecting on the Bay less prolific.

This small sampling of shards from the upper half of Maryland's Eastern Shore of the Chesapeake was collected between 1999 and 2010. Note that the Eastern Shore faces westward across the Bay and the Western Shore faces eastward. This gathering mostly displays bottle pieces from the first half of the 20th century, with a few earlier samples.

On the top left is a rare turquoise-blue, Milk-Glass shard from a creamer or sugar bowl. Next to it are aqua-colored collar shards from Ball Mason jars and, further right, a piece of pale green, Jadeite tableware. At the bottom right, there's a soft pink piece of Depression glass. These were all popular during the 1930s to 1950s. The two rarest shards are in the center—a deep pink, Cranberry Opalescent piece of layered glass, possibly by Fenton Glass in the late 1940s or 1950s, and a bright yellow shard to its left. The yellow piece is layered glass with a snow-white inside liner and was likely a lamp shade cover or decorative vase. Just below it is the base of a wine goblet or tumbler with a starburst pattern.

Up top, there's a vestige of a soft green bottle base with an open pontil scar in the center. While the scar places it prior to 1860, the bubbly glass core leads one to believe it's older. Near it are several black glass shards. These are similar to thick sections of late-1800 beer bottles formed not long before the teal-green pieces, a popular bottle color in the 1880s and 1890s. The soft blue piece, right of center, has a unique pattern similar to a 1860s Cathedral-style pickle jar. The cobalt blues are likely from the nearby Bromo-Seltzer plant and cornflower blue from a Phillips' Milk of Magnesia bottle.

This image presents colors uncommon today that were once extremely common in the late 1800s and early 1900s. An abundance of glass objects were cast off by staff at a thriving Chesapeake Bay amusement park during busy summer weekends. Thousands of soda and beer bottles were scrapped, as well as occasional stomach and headache remedies. From 1890 to 1910, the most prevalent colors for beverage containers were soft blue and soft green. Meanwhile, most food and other beverage containers made of clear glass at that time turned light purple with sunlight. After the turn of the century, mass-produced bottles for medicines and poisons were routinely formed in cobalt blue. The purpose of this image is to capture colors at the start of the industrial age— as our country outgrew mouth-blown vessels and entered automation. By 1920, producers had removed manganese from the production of clear glass allowing it to stay clear over time. Manufacturers began to focus on common green and brown glass for production bottles, with few variations for the next 90 years.

Sea glass collection courtesy of Richard and Nancy LaMotte – Eastern Shore of Chesapeake Bay

Chesapeake Bay, Maryland
WESTERN SHORE

Not far downriver from the location where a captive Francis Scott Key drafted our national anthem are some small, uninviting beaches that retain glass remnants from Baltimore's past. Several objects are rarely found elsewhere, especially on coastal waters. One shown in the prior chapter included fragments of a unique, footed seltzer bottle in stunning turquoise blue. The Baltimore region represents a significant place in the history of our country, so finding shards from 1960 near shards from 1760 is not uncommon. The Port of Baltimore was formally established in 1706, although settlers already in Baltimore had been using the Patapsco River for trade at least 50 years earlier.

The two bulbous rings in the center are blob-top-style lip shards from soda and beer bottles popular in the 1860s to 1880s. The deep olive-green blob top is the rarer of the two and could have been produced at the nearby Baltimore Glass Works. The large black, glass-bottle base in the upper left is a piece of a thick Bitterquelle bottle from the same time period. The lip shard on the lower left and the neck shard on the upper right are both circa mid- to late 1700s. By contrast, at left is a cornflower-blue shard showing a strap-style sidewall, a common mold design on Milk of Magnesia bottles in the early 1900s. The decorative cobalt-blue shard in the center and one on the far right could be from early 20th-century poison bottles. The very thick cobalt-blue piece at top is perhaps from the shoulder of a blob-top soda bottle of the 1860 to 1880 time period. On the bottom right is a cobalt-blue, light-bulb insulator, found with part of its aluminum thread still intact. Directly left is half of an older black amethyst version of the same insulator. Besides the insulators, the remainder of this gathering is from bottle glass.

The next collection of rare objects is highlighted by a stunning red-orange finial often on the top of an early 1900s candy jar lid. Beneath it is a soft pink base to a drinking glass probably from a Depression-glass set. The curious items at left include a rod-in-hand, pressed-glass piece perhaps from a serving tray handle. Above it is an odd, two-toned piece of art glass, possibly part of a molded souvenir cup or vase. The very small hole molded into the yellow-green shard is where a metal handle would have been mounted. Decorative miniature coal scuttles used as ashtrays or to hold matches from the 1930s to 1950s had this feature. Beneath them is a more common base to a milk-glass jar that would have held cold cream or toothpaste.

In some cases, large five-gallon, water-cooler bottles and carboys would have cracked-ice-style embossing on their base. These two large, very thick shards are likely from one of those containers produced early in the 20th century.

Sea glass collection courtesy of Stu and Emily Jacobs – Western Shore of the Chesapeake Bay

Outer Banks, North Carolina

The Outer Banks of North Carolina stretch more than half the length of the entire state. Like many remote coastal enclaves, this isolated band of dunes started as a retreat from inland heat and mosquitoes and then became host to fishing villages before the mid-1800s. By the 1850s, Nags Head had become one of the original beach vacation towns in the region. As the popularity of the Outer Banks grew, the town also became a summer destination for America's greatest jazz musicians and singers. By the late 1930s, entertainers like Duke Ellington, Louis Armstrong, Count Basie, and Fats Domino performed at the Nags Head Casino and paved the way for later groups such as the Embers, Drifters, Platters, and more. Hotels flourished in the early years and then gave way to private homes that blanket the dunes today.

The objects in this image reflect goods primarily used during the late 1800s to early 1900s, even though they were collected at Nags Head during the late 20th century. The only modern piece in this image is the six-sided base of a beer mug, a rare find since such sturdy vessels would normally require a rather severe impact to be rendered unusable. The lavender stopper would have originally held a cork sheath on its shaft and was possibly used to seal a 1890s era patent-medicine or sauce container. The remaining shards in this image, each showing lavender colorations, are also remnants of patent-medicine-style containers. They display the pre-1915 purple hue created from solar oxidation of the manganese within its core. The heavily pinched-up and asymmetrical bottle bottom on the far left indicates a crude hand-blown vessel, as does the double-tapered wall shard up top. The neck shard in the upper right is a common design for late 19th-century patent-medicine-style containers.

Outer Banks, North Carolina

The image with native Carolina sand highlights two centuries of glass. The two, black glass pieces have bubbling through their core and resemble portions of 18th-century wine bottles. The thick one in the foreground shows hints of iron oxidation releasing from its pitted surface. Iron was a common colorant used to darken glass during that era. The rounded shape of this shard seems to be part of an onion-style wine bottle from the 1700s.

The remaining white and soft blue or green pieces are from 1900 to the 1950s, with the most recent being the ribbed shard on the lower left from a food container such as a honey jar. Above it is a portion of a clear jug handle. The longer, soft green handle above that is more likely a pitcher handle from the 1920s or 1930s. Further above is a postage-stamp-sized sampler bottle, possibly for perfume.

The extremely odd object in the center was in a beach campfire, as evidenced by the small black specks embedded in its surface. It most closely resembles a glass-fuse enclosure from inside a light bulb. On the upper right is a flat piece of window glass, a medicine-bottle neck, and two bottle bottoms. The soft green shard at the bottom is likely from an early 1900s soda bottle. The white one shows a suction scar, a mold mark common on bottles from the 1920s, this one possibly on a half-pint of whisky.

Florida

The west coast of Florida has a reputation for superb shelling beaches but not for finding sea glass. Years ago, its east coast yielded reliable supplies of sea glass from Vero Beach to Jacksonville. However, sea glass is now difficult to find along both coasts of the Sunshine state. Shards of glass found today normally show less wear on their edges, since the soft coral sand does not abrade them as aggressively as sand in the coarse littoral zones of the northeast.

These shards from the Vero Beach region show a bold cobalt-blue bottle bottom embossed "Salvitae American Apothecaries Co New York." It is fortunate this part of the bottle was found since the remainder of the bottle had no embossing; it was branded only with a paper label. The company registered a trademark for their product and marketed it as an uric acid eliminator for rheumatism and gout in 1905. One of their many claims was, "Salvitae prevents premature fossilization of the individual." Its mixture of strontium, lithium, caffeine, quinine, and other suspect ingredients made for an interesting oral remedy.

The other cobalt-blue shard was an insulator from the base of a rather large light bulb, since its diameter was approximately 1 1/2 inches—most are only 1 inch or less. Just to its right, there's a thick tapering milk-bottle lip with a well-defined inside ledge known as a "capseat," where the wax-wafer seal was secured. These bottles were delivered to the doorstep of many homes in the first half of the 20th century.

Another popular item expended during that era was Coca-Cola® bottles. Here a complete Crown Cork closure lip and collar has a piece of coral wedged in its mouth. Another Coke bottle wall shard is on the far right.

The very pale, white-green shard in the center is a uniquely severe kick-up from the bottom edge of a turn-of-the-20th-century wine or sauce bottle. Other than the blue-green Coke shards, the assorted soft blues are good examples of common bottles produced from the very late 19th to early 20th centuries. The bold green pieces are from recent beverages, while the pale greens are possibly from wine or cooking oil bottles.

Sea glass collection courtesy of A. J. and Kimberly Koontz – Treasure Coast, Vero Beach, Florida

Texas

Sea glass has always been a challenge to find along the Gulf of Mexico. While Floridians barely locate any there today, collectors in the Galveston, Texas, region have been gathering shards more routinely. An assortment of debris washed ashore for many decades following the devastating Galveston hurricane in September of 1900 that took 8,000 lives. This collection, mostly from beaches just south of Galveston, includes a number of more recent shards from the early to mid-1900s. One key is the post-1933, Clorox quart-bottle shard at the top left. Another is the Owens-Illinois bottle bottom in the foreground with its diamond-O logo, likely from a half-pint whiskey bottle. The latter is from the 1950s or '60s due to the stippling pattern across the bottom. The amber screw-cap bottle lip and neck to its right is perchance the upper portion of the same type of vessel.

The eldest fragments are the soft lavender-colored piece from a pre-1915 strap flask and the very pale blue shard in front. The two clear glass items are likely post-1920, since they show no sign of manganese that slowly purples old glass. The golden-amber and Kelly-green pieces are from more recent beverages.

The ceramic piece at top displays the white foot of a dinner plate, and its varied green-colored pattern appears much like vintage Majolica ware.

Sea glass collection courtesy of Jody Diehl of Beach Treasures, treasurebeaches.com – Galveston, Texas

Southern California

Halfway between Los Angeles and San Diego are an assortment of beaches that have yielded plentiful sea glass over the years. A collector in the San Clemente region has been able to obtain a wide variety of bottle and tableware pieces exhibiting features common to items produced in the early and mid-1900s. Since San Clemente was developed primarily after 1925, this explains why little pre-1900 glass is found.

The ceramics with boldly colored surfaces in the lower portion of this image are from Fiestaware. Introduced by The Homer Laughlin China Company in 1936, the initial Fiesta® pattern was available in five colors—red, yellow, cobalt blue, light green, and ivory. The next year, they introduced turquoise blue. The worn cobalt-blue shard in the foreground was likely produced between 1936 and 1951. The light green and turquoise pieces above it are perhaps the same age. Fiestaware was popular during the 1930s and '40s, and the pastel tones sold quite well during the 1950s. The pattern was retired in late 1972 but returned to production in 1986. Note many of Fiestaware's pastel colors are similar to traditional sea-glass colors.

Just above the Fiestaware is a unique and well-tumbled tricolor piece of campfire glass with charred remnants embedded in its surface. Lower to the left is an even rarer shard of cobalt-blue-and-white campfire glass. Both items fused together either at a seaside campfire or at a dump where fires were regularly lit to reduce the height of unwanted refuse.

Near the top of the image is a pale-green shard of Jadeite ceramic tableware. Two pieces of glass are also from tableware items, including the rare yellow shard in the lower right. The large gray shard in the middle is from leaded glass oxidized to a soft gray hue after years of exposure to sunlight. The remaining shards are mostly from modern bottles, such as the jade greens in the upper left and cobalt blues in the foreground. On the far right is a wall shard of a mid-1900s Coca-Cola bottle displaying its soft green tone and fluted, hobble-skirt pattern.

The iridescent pieces of the abalone shell are a striking contrast to the muted pastels of sea glass. The shells of these colorful sea snails have been used in jewelry and buttons, as well as inlays on furniture and musical instruments. Finding abalone shells in southern California is more challenging than northern California. Overharvesting and storms, which ruined the southern California kelp beds on which the abalone feed, nearly depleted their population by 1970. The state later created regulations to reduce commercial collection of abalone in California.

Sea glass collection courtesy of Lori Lambert, Adornment – Capistrano Beach, California

Central Coast, California
MONTEREY BAY

Along the California coast, there is remarkable diversity among their sea-glass sites. The popular "Glass Beach" at Fort Bragg has been taken over by the state; another is too treacherous for the average collector to access, while one more is on the brink of being lost to development. Nevertheless, a very rich history echoes from the town of Monterey where barking sea lions serenade sleepless tourists along Cannery Row. Once the Spanish capital city for California back in 1776, Monterey didn't become part of the United States officially until 1850.

Finding 200-year-old shards in this region is far less likely than finding colonial relics on Bermuda or along the eastern seaboard. However, as with many sea-glass beaches, collecting after a storm is frequently more productive, especially along shorelines previously used as landfills or dumps. These unique locations can yield very diverse colors and shapes of sea glass that change daily due to the vast array of tableware items discarded over the years.

The dark round shard in the upper left corner of this photo is actually the base to a Royal Ruby red tumbler (drinking glass). It is not embossed, so it's not part of a rare Royal Ruby Schlitz bottle. Leaning on it is a Depression-glass handle to a creamer or teacup with a pastel lime color from low-levels of uranium, making it fluoresce to a light yellow under a UV light. Below it are several peach-colored shards of Depression-glass tableware. In the center are some lemon-yellow pieces from tableware of the same era.

Many collectors seek red sea glass but very few ever find an antique glass tail light with a marbled surface. This classic is likely from an old Dodge truck circa 1930s to 1940s. Leaning on it is a cobalt-blue bottle shard possibly from San Francisco's Owl Drug Company, a popular producer of medicines in cobalt-blue bottles in the early 1900s. The latter medication was perhaps consumed by a despondent truck driver after wrecking his 1930s Dodge!

The iridescent abalone shells are from native abalone mollusks in the central California coast. Here the abalone are mostly farm-raised in shoreline beds where the rarity of strong storms in this region creates an ideal setting to grow these fragile creatures. The overall lack of frequent storms and soft sands of the littoral zone inside Monterey Bay provide clues to why shards here are slowly buffed and worn.

Sea glass collection courtesy of Jayne Hawley – Monterey Bay, California

Sea glass collection courtesy of Santa Cruz Sea Glass – Davenport Beach, California

Central Coast, California
SANTA CRUZ

In the late 1860s, a small coastal village was started just north of Santa Cruz, California. The town was named for Rhode Island sea captain John Davenport, who moved there to begin his own whaling and lumber business. He built a large wharf and supplied timber to San Francisco into the 1880s. One large business after another seemed to flourish for a few short decades and then later declined. However, Davenport succeeded in retaining its small and somewhat reclusive appeal.

One small enterprise that has endured several challenges since opening in 1970 is the local art-glass studio of James Lundberg. He specialized in various styles of decorative glass from Art Deco to Tiffany forms, and portions of his exquisite vases, lighting fixtures, and paperweights have made their way into museums across America. Lundberg spent 22 years perfecting his expertise but was tragically killed while riding a bike. Fortunately, his wife continues to keep the business moving forward.

A few years after Lundberg started his business, flood waters came down the nearby stream and washed away a large portion of his trimmings along with slag (opaque pressed glass with colored streaks) staged behind the building. The stream fed into the ocean, and about 30 years later, surfers began noticing tumbled glass fragments on a secluded cliff-side beach. These were clearly not from production glass.

The shards shown here are some of the trimmings from the mid-1970s flood that carried scrap Lundberg glass into the Pacific. These multi-colored gems are the most unique sea glass in North America, if not on the globe. Most are layered glass from objects discarded as scrap or cut from composite rods used while crafting finished goods. The trimmings that appear like mushrooms or stoppers were likely snipped from the ends of lamp shades or vases. The round cobalt-blue-edged rings with translucent white cores are cut from rods of bull's eye murrini (glass cross-sections of colored patterns). At left, the green fern-leaf pattern was used to decorate some vases.

Much of the collection looks like candy. Those who recall Beech Nut's classic Fruit Stripe gum from the 1960s may be drawn to the striped shard in the center and one in the upper left. Before attempting to find some of the few remaining Lundberg pieces in Davenport, note the cliff-side beach is dangerous to reach and supplies are virtually exhausted. Few of these unique nuggets still remain as artists and collectors have done an admirable job of cleaning the shoreline.

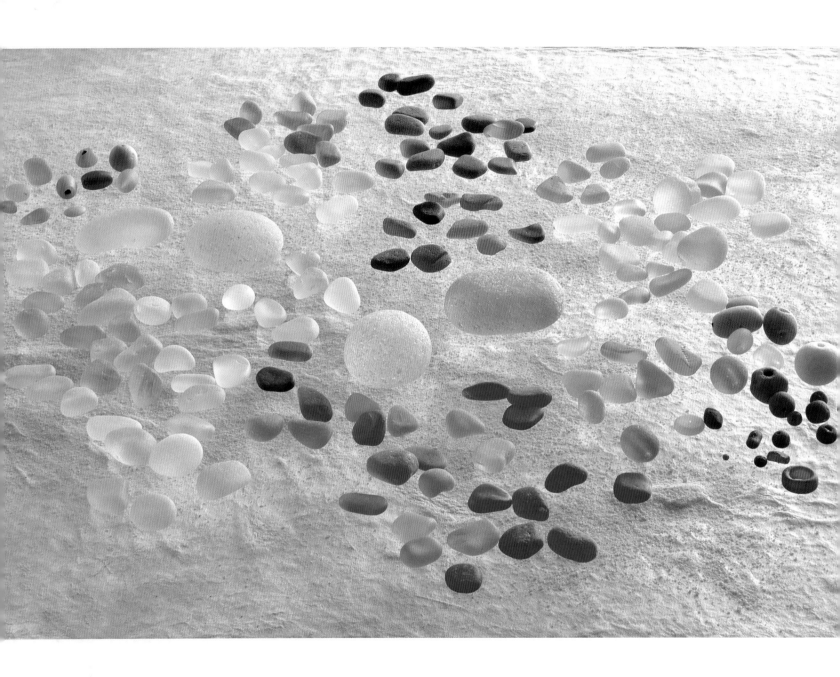

Pacific Northwest, Washington

The aggressive shorelines of the Pacific Northwest tend to cure glass objects of their sheen and sharp edges faster than most beaches to their south. Along the Strait of Juan de Fuca, swift tides and wind-driven surface waters combine with vast shipping traffic to create one of nature's most efficient sea-glass conditioning environments.

As indicated in this image, an observer can see that shards customary to this region are more worn, rounded, and smaller than those of similar age found in other locations. The text and identifying marks on these petite fragments are quickly erased, their origins far more difficult to ascertain beyond assessing colors common to objects during specific time periods.

The cobalt blue and cornflower blues are most likely from Milk of Magnesia bottles or similar vessels for medical treatments in the early to mid-1900s. The soft blue shards to the left are from soda and beer bottles of the early 1900s, but the larger rounded pieces are fragments of insulators. The turquoise scraps are apt to be from specialty tableware or a rare mineral-water bottle. Other than the green and amber latter-day bottle shards up top, there are significant signs of tableware in this collection.

Observing the two bulbous pieces in the center, the white appears to be part of a decanter stopper or finial, while the gray piece just to the right is sun-colored leaded glass, again likely from tableware. The soft pink or peach shards are mostly Depression-glass items alongside sun-colored, amethyst shards from bottles dating between 1875 and 1915. The abundance of orange, red, and yellow pieces boldly identifies the source as a dump site, since many are from signal lights and tableware.

One benefit to scouring this region's beaches is the abundance of beads to be found. The Pacific Northwest was once a melting pot of travelers bringing trading and decorative beads from China and Russia, as well as from Europe after the 1700s. In the early 1800s, it was already clear to traders from the Far East that some local Native American Indians preferred the blue and white beads far more than red ones. The "Russian Blue" beads, similar to one shown at the far left, were often traded to Indians in exchange for furs. Today, some red beads are also found from lost fishing lures. The mysteries behind the ages and origins of beads are a fascinating history lesson.

Other beach treasures contributed by fishermen are the glass fishing floats that travel the Pacific arriving from Japan. These unique glass balls are used to support fishing nets, and while some reach Washington and Oregon beaches intact, many are shattered. While it's not easy to identify typical wall shards on these orbs, the seal—known to collectors as the button—often has an embossed logo. Most of these are ball-shaped, but other forms include egg and rolling-pin versions. The shard at right is the inner portion of the seal from a large fishing float.

Pacific Northwest, Washington

An example of typical wear on Northwestern shards is shown in this image. The two larger white pieces are likely from the heads of decanter stoppers, but the smaller one at left could be a finial on the lid of a cookie jar or sugar bowl. The bright pink stopper in the middle was perhaps the head of a perfume dauber, since the color is richer than the soft pink color used in Depression glass. The more peach-colored finial below it, more closely matches a finial on a Depression-glass jar lid.

Great Lakes, Michigan

The southern shores of Lake Michigan have been productive areas for sea glass for at least 100 years. From Racine, Wisconsin, to South Haven, Michigan, and points north, there are sands that still hide fragments of the region's past. This particular assemblage of glass is from the northern section of Lake Michigan, collected on secluded Beaver Island.

Originally a settlement for Native American Indians in the 1700s, Beaver Island became a haven for a group of Mormons who settled there in the mid-1800s until its zealous leader was assassinated. Soon afterward, his followers were replaced primarily by Irish fishermen, lured by the rich fishing grounds nearby. But then, well before the turn of the 20th century, automated fishing vessels from mainland ports nearly wiped out their once bountiful livelihood, along with many fisheries within the Great Lakes. By the early 1900s, Beaver Island transitioned, this time into a major lumber supplier to Detroit and Chicago. When that industry shut down in 1916, the island struggled again to survive until tourism finally took hold in the 1970s. Reviewing this island's intriguing history may cause some to reflect on our harsh treatment of coastal resources.

Most of the glass objects shown here were discarded during the island's boom years of the late 1800s and early 1900s. For example, the soft blue bottle bottom in the upper left is embossed with E.R. Durkee & Co New York. This is likely from their 1890-1900 era, beehive-shaped condiment sauce bottle, since later versions were predominantly clear. The Durkee Company was founded in 1850 in Buffalo and then moved to the New York City region. By 1906, Durkee held one of the first patented salad dressings in the United States. At a time when the government began an extensive crackdown on food suppliers for false claims, Durkee's honestly crafted product lines helped them earn and maintain a reputation for their "pure" ingredients.

Another item potentially from the late 1800s is the purple shard in the foreground showing three scalloped edges, common on student-style lamp shades made for oil lamps during that period. Some collectors also find shards of these in "cased" form, layered with white glass on the inside. Leaning on the purple shard is a unique electrical covering in clear glass. The remaining sun-colored lavender shards up top indicate pre-1915 glassware, but the deep purple piece at left was apparently a decorative piece of pressed glass from the late 1800s to early 1900s.

Four aqua shards displaying large ribs are collar pieces from Mason Jars from the first half of the 20th century. The other aqua items are plausibly from the same containers. The bold green shard is from a circa 1960s gallon jug handle.

The thick, dark gray shard in the upper left and the peacock-blue one in front are extremely unusual colors. While leaded glass can produce a sun-colored gray cast, this one appears to have other metal oxidation within its core, possibly from copper. This color is seen at times on vintage-glass battery encasements; the peacock blue is more likely an off-color of what was to be cobalt blue for some medicinal bottle. Not every bottle color produced prior to automation held an identical hue.

The unmistakable "M" milk-bottle bottom in the center offers several clues to its age. The circular valve mark in its center was consistently on milk bottles during the 1920s to 1940s. The bold embossed letter on milk bottles was to identify the dairy since these vessels were on loan to their customers. The challenge is ascertaining the specific dairy, since many local dairies in Michigan were operated by families, or named for towns, beginning with the letter M.

Sea glass collection of Annette Dashiell – Beaver Island, Michigan

Sea glass collection courtesy of Terri and Jennifer Reed of Relish, Inc. – Lake Erie, Pennsylvania

Great Lakes — Erie

Many of the wind-swept shorelines of the Great Lakes are lined with pebbles and stones which normally abrade sea glass into small fragments. Each of the Lakes has popular spots for sea-glass collectors, especially near active ports that served industry and tourists back in the late 1800s and early 1900s.

A collector who found an abundance of identical soft green glass marbles washed up near a port in Racine, Wisconsin, later traced them to an old bottling plant. Remnants of light-bulb insulators and some bulk-slag glass along the shore of Lake Erie have been credited to a large General Electric production plant on Lake Erie's shoreline in Ohio. Frequent on-shore winds return many of our glass castaways back to American shores, but the popularity of sea glass in this 21st century has meant fewer shards and smaller sizes for all to find.

In this collection from Erie, Pennsylvania, one is drawn to the piercing eyes of a clear glass baby doll head. The sparse bundle of hair on top is the key feature of a pixie cartoon character known as the "Kewpie doll." Initially an illustration by Rose O'Neill for *Ladies Home Journal* in 1909, the Kewpie doll, with its tiny wings, was extremely popular in the first half of the 20th century. First produced in bisque and celluloid (plastic), this clear glass version was actually part of the handle on a Depression-glass dinner bell.

To the far right, another rarity is an orange glass cat. Miniature antique Czech-glass Christmas "cracker" charms were often made as small dogs and cats but were primarily produced in black. Hidden within these celebratory pull-apart poppers known as crackers, the small glass charms were popular during the 1920s and 1930s. They often came with small metal collars for attachment to necklaces and bracelets.

The toy dice are also exceptional finds since undamaged whole items are not discarded regularly. Sea-glass collectors will occasionally find toy marbles, but pressed-glass dice are far scarcer. The buffed green button at the top is pressed glass and appears to be early 20th century. The black button, lying face down, is quite likely Victorian.

The round signal reflectors were mounted on stop signs and railroad-crossing signs for safety in the 1920s and 1930s and also later adorned bicycles. Green reflectors were used primarily for railroad directional signage. Above them, the acorn-shaped red reflector is a Cataphote-style known as a Cat-eye, which were embedded onto roads and used as signs. A similar form known as the "Glo-Brite" reflector was also on some motorcycles and autos during that era. Glass reflectors have provided safety for evening travel since the early 1900s, but most have been replaced with plastic today.

Lake Erie Slag Glass

One of the most challenging types of sea glass to identify and date is amorphous, raw-production slag from glass factories. This is commonly referred to as "end-of-day" glass and can sometimes be found with mixed colors if one color was being added to flush out an existing color from molten pots or processing equipment. These large chunks of glass should not be confused with bonfire glass that is usually thinner, smaller, and routinely has specs of black soot or sand embedded on the surface.

One unique location where collectors have found abundant pieces of slag glass is along the south shore of Lake Erie near Conneaut, Ohio. Mostly seen in deep cobalt blue or black amethyst, the slag found there runs in size from eggs to avocados. Locals determined these were from the nearby General Electric plant that used the dark glass in the base of light bulbs as insulators. It has been reported that some slag was purposefully used to prevent beach erosion. The plant was opened in 1941, but along with five other GE plants in northeastern Ohio, it was closed in 2008 when it became clear domestic production of incandescent bulbs was to be eliminated by 2014.

"STUDENTS OF
AMERICAN GLASS
MUST ALWAYS KEEP
IN MIND THAT THE
CREATIONS THEY
COLLECT ARE TRULY
EXAMPLES OF OUR
AMERICAN CULTURE...
AND THUS HAVE
HISTORICAL
SIGNIFICANCE."

— JAMES LAFFERTY

IDENTIFYING PIECES
OF OUR PAST

Identification and Dating

Excellent resources for assisting bottle collectors or amateur archaeologists are evolving on the internet. Those websites can also help sea-glass collectors identify their shards. One specifically on bottle identification is operated by the Society for Historical Archaeology and has excellent educational content and images. But there is never a substitute for experience. A young bottle collector can only rarely outguess a seasoned veteran who has been hunting, digging, buying, and selling antique bottles for 30 years. Firsthand observation of actual vessels during a bottle show or at an antique store provides far more than just a glimpse into the details that separate 20th-century glass from earlier forms. A basic introduction to determining the history of a shard was presented in the *Pure Sea Glass* book and its identification card deck. This chapter is designed to help increase one's knowledge by sharing insight on several of the unique pieces presented by collectors over the years. Most are uncommon and are shown to help other collectors learn how to look for clues, so they can search for history within their own collections.

COLOR, FORM, MARKINGS, AND CORE

When bending to lift a shard from the edge of the shore, the collector's immediate first assessment is to determine its color. In some cases, they find out that one color appears different indoors than it did in the bright outdoor sun. For those who don't suffer from color-blindness, this is also the initial appraisal of its value to us. A very rare color can excite a collector to a point where they make audible remarks and find creative ways to secure their find for the trip home. Identifying and dating the shard is a bit more complicated. The form is usually the next feature assessed. Sea-glass collectors, of course, want a well-worn shard, but that often makes identification even more challenging. Feel the shard and determine if it has any rounded features common with bottles. Flat pieces of pane glass or tableware can be laid down on a level surface, and if all the edges directly contact that surface, it is usually not from a bottle. However, if the shard is flat but has variable thickness, then it is still likely part of a bottle. There were a number of flat-sided bottles produced by 1900, but in comparison to bottle shards with rounded features, the numbers are small. A light blue shard, perfectly flat on both sides with a uniform thickness of roughly 1/4 inch, is often from a window, while a thinner one closer to 1/8 inch can be from picture frame glass. Flat bottle fragments normally have some contour and variable thickness. By studying bottles one can begin to get a feel for whether a shard is part of the shoulder, heel, neck, or collar. The collector who wants to broaden their identification skills should search for local bottle shows within their region. One of the premier annual bottle shows in the U.S. is the Baltimore Bottle Show held in early March, but most states have their own annual events.

After concluding a color and form examination, look closely at the piece for any sign of text. Bottle glass prior to the second half of the 19th century rarely had any embossed text or numbers. It was in the mid-1800s when molds began to include thick crude lettering on the bases and sides of bottles. That bold and rudimentary lettering is not nearly as refined as the text on 20th-century bottles, when automated molds took over. A premier reference for identification of makers' marks embossed on bottles of the late 19th to mid-20th century is Julian Toulouse's *Bottle Makers and Their Marks*. If a bottle bottom shard displays a tread-like pattern along its perimeter or dotted (stippling) pattern on its base, it was likely produced in the second half of the 20th century. Those odd marks, still in use today, were to help optimize production as bottles moved down conveyor lines from the molds to the annealing ovens.

To get a feel for the age of the glass, examine the core clarity within the glass. To do this, hold a bright light behind the shard to inspect the glass for bubbles or internal cloudiness. In general, 18th-century bottle glass in olive-green or soft blue color tones will have a hazier core and routinely has excessive core bubbling commonly referred to as "seeds" in the glass. Some glass during that period, produced by more patient glassmakers, may show few bubbles. By the mid-19th century, bubbles within the glass were greatly reduced, but large bubbles could be seen sporadically. By the early 20th century, automated bottle machinery virtually eliminated the presence of bubbles in mass-produced bottles. Some common exceptions are hastily made Mason jars from the early 1900s, which are found with a few large bubbles.

Keep in mind that shards of the most common—and even some uncommon—colors are from bottles, while the extremely rare colors most likely derive from other sources. Learning to identify and date shards within your own collection can be quite rewarding. Sharing that talent, uncovering historical mysteries with family and friends can be even more gratifying.

Colonial Glass and Pottery
LEWES SHIPWRECK

On a cool winter wind in early 1774, a three-masted sailing vessel left port from Bristol, England bound for Philadelphia. It was loaded with goods created by German and Dutch craftsmen since items of British manufacture carried tariffs unpopular with American colonists. After a long voyage, the captain and crew of the ship Severn found themselves entering Delaware Bay on May 4th during a rare spring snowstorm. The captain elected to steer his ship toward shore and ran aground at the entry to Roosevelt Inlet in Lewes, Delaware. Fortunately, by landing in less deep water, the crew survived, and some of the cargo was salvaged, but a large portion ended up on the floor of the Bay.

After 230 years underwater, the previously undisturbed colonial artifacts finally reached land but as fragments of their former selves. These appeared on the shores of Lewes Beach in September of 2004. Their arrival was in abundance, the beach was abruptly littered with thousands of dark, olive-green glass shards from 18th-century bottles. They were accompanied by an assortment of stoneware and earthenware shards along with razor-thin pieces of aqua flat glass. Beachcombers hastily collected all they could secure, and soon local authorities closed off a section of the shore to protect it for an archaeological study. It was quickly determined that a dredging vessel, hired to siphon sand from the bottom of the Bay for a beach replenishment project, had extracted objects from a sunken ship.

A year later, archaeologists and historians finally agreed these were from the wreck of the Severn which had crossed the ocean and been abandoned not far south of its port of call, Philadelphia. It's unclear how much of the original cargo was salvaged but is clear that a large amount went down with the ship.

This sampling of the blue and gray German Rhenish ware was known as Westerwald stoneware. Lying with it are some shards of Delft blue earthenware, its tin-glazed layer of blue and white noticeably flaked away from its tan paste. Also shown are two pipe stems and about a dozen pieces of Frankfurter stoneware, known for its yellow and green lead-glazed interior.

Colonial Glass and Pottery: Lewes Shipwreck

An additional assemblage shows olive-green bottle glass along with pale flat shards of almost paper-thin, Crown window glass that would have been shipped as large round disks and cut to size by local craftsman. The thick, curvy olive-green shards were from onion-shaped wine bottles, including one entire lip found intact with its cork. The slightly thinner, flat and boxy, dark olive pieces were from an abundance of Case Gin bottles whose sturdy wooden boxes ultimately failed to protect their neatly organized payload after centuries below the surface.

None of the items exhibited signs of wear common to genuine sea glass; nevertheless, the close-knit community of Lewes became captivated with their sudden bounty. In an uncharacteristic move by a state or local archaeological project, officials actually enlisted the assistance of those who collected shards to donate and help catalog the fragments. This, along with a dive to the site 15 feet below the surface greatly aided the process of narrowing down which ship had been uncovered. After some 40,000 shards were collected, the task force assigned to the study told collectors they could now keep everything they find. The project was complete, and the Severn was allowed to rest quietly as a National Historic Landmark.

Insulators

Glass has long been recognized as an effective protector to insulate other materials from electrical current. One early application was for lightning-rod insulators to protect homes. By the 1850s, beehive-shaped glass insulators produced by companies like Hemingray were being used on telegraph poles. Hemingray, of Covington, Kentucky, became the dominant manufacturer. Brookfield was another large producer, which began making the first screw-thread insulators in the late 1860s and embossed the Brookfield name on them from 1869 to 1909. As electricity grew in popularity in the late 1880s, the need for more stable insulators led Hemingray to patent a drip-points design in 1893 to reduce moisture from rotting the wooden mounting pin. Collectors who find shards from electric and communication insulators often see the inside thread design as shown in the top of this photo. The cobalt-blue insulator is far rarer and quite collectible. The growth of electric lines through the U.S. was strong in the early 1900s but really escalated in the late 1930s from the Rural Electrification Act. In the 1950s, porcelain insulators became common, and production of glass insulators virtually stopped by 1970.

Shards that appear like black-amethyst or cobalt-blue buttons with a large center are actually insulators from the bottom of light bulbs. These are concealed within the base of the metal screw thread we twist into sockets at home. The button-shaped disks are found in areas where household refuse was discarded, especially in the first half of the 20th century. It was late in 1879 when Thomas Edison first lit an incandescent bulb. He designed the screw-in base in 1881 and merged his Edison Electric Company with Thomson-Houston in 1892, creating what would soon become General Electric. The design survived with only minor changes until recently, when production was outlawed in favor of energy saving compact fluorescent bulbs.

While several black-amethyst light bulb insulators exhibit crude features like bubbles and uneven shapes, as in the foreground of this image, the cobalt-blue insulators were assumed to be more modern. But the antique light bulb shown on this page has a vibrant cobalt-blue insulator. Thus, dating light bulb insulators is no easy task.

Wash Boards

Uniformly ribbed and textured glass shards, perfectly flat on their reverse sides, are often from antique glass washboards used to scrub clothes in a soaking bucket. In this country, they evolved from all-wooden washboards with crudely cut grooves in the early 19th century to rugged boards of fluted tin patented by Stephen Rust in 1833. Other metals were also popular, such as zinc and galvanized steel. Some were coated in rubber in the 1850s before pressed-glass and ceramic washboards were developed in the late 1870s.

The popularity of washboards waned quickly following the advent of washing machines in the late 1920s and early 1930s. While it is unclear when glass washboards went out of style, the metal versions found great favor with musicians in the 1920s. Those were especially popular in the southern Cajun-style bands and can still be seen in use in New Orleans clubs.

Today the Columbus Washboard Company remains as one of the few producers of original glass washboards. What is even more noteworthy is what they provide for enlisted U.S. military personnel. Citizens can send a metal washboard Troop Kit to active duty military personnel anywhere in the world at the company's cost with shipping included.

Turtle Ink Wells

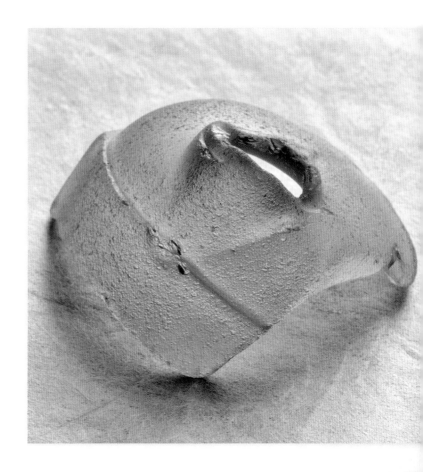

A rounded shard with a small open orifice, similar to the one shown here, could be mistaken for an oil lamp, target ball, or several other glass objects. But the location of this opening next to a sturdy shoulder seam helps identify this particular shard as the top half of what is called a "turtle" or "igloo" ink bottle.

Most turtle inkwells were produced from the late 1860s to early 1900s in translucent aqua blue, similar to the full-sized bottle illustrated here. Its markings on the sidewall display "J & IE Moore" of Warren, Massachusetts. Their firm is recognized as one of the largest domestic producers of these forms. This yellow-green-toned, citron color is significantly rarer than the more common aqua bottles.

Low-profile vessels were popular in schools, presumably to limit desk spills. Earlier models were a bit more upright, and, prior to the 1800s, most inkwells were produced in sturdy stoneware. A feather quill was used to deliver the ink to paper until the late 1850s, when metal, split-tipped pens were developed.

The prolific inkwell began to lose popularity when fountain pens were developed in the 1880s. By the 1940s, the first ballpoint pens helped bring affordable writing utensils to the masses.

A n amber shard that appears like stacked logs could be a remnant of the once popular Drake's Plantation Bitters bottle molded in the shape of a log cabin. The design was patented by Patrick Henry Drake in 1862 and produced in New York. Most were created in medium amber hues, some also in dark red amber, citron green and golden amber. Once shipped throughout the U.S. in high volumes, shards from this bottle are rarely found. Similar later versions include Old Cabin Bitters, Kelly's Log Cabin Bitters and American Life Bitters. A mix of herbs and alcohol, bitters were popular beverages with soldiers during the Civil War and used to avoid regulations on straight liquors.

Baking Powder

One quite common bottle produced and discarded during the late 19th century was the short, wide-mouthed vessel used for baking powder. The largest domestic producer at the time was Rhode Island's Rumford Chemical Works, whose baking powder is still available in cans on grocery store shelves. It was started in the 1850s by Harvard Professor Eben Horsford who developed a calcium acid phosphate compound with sodium bicarbonate for self-rising flour. In 1869, Horsford added corn starch as a key drying agent for stability, and these three ingredients remain essential to the product even today. Horsford named the company after the academic post he held in organic chemistry at Harvard, the Rumford Chair. He is credited with a vast number of inventions that aided society and the military and was an early champion of establishing scientific laboratories in educational institutions.

By the late 1800s, Rumford Baking Powder was being sold throughout the country as well as overseas. Another prevalent producer was the R. B. Davis and Company of Hoboken, New Jersey. Their "Davis OK"-branded Baking Powder bottles were nearly identical to the classic Rumford glass containers. Found today, these two forms are so abundant that antique bottle collectors often treat them with nonchalance, similar to the feelings of a veteran sea-glass collector toward finding an unworn white shard.

The good news for sea-glass collectors is that these vessels were used in mass volumes during the late 19th and early 20th centuries when stock glass colors were translucent soft blue, soft green, and, occasionally, teal. While lip and neck shards can be easily identified as coming from those general containers, it is the bold shoulder embossing for "Davis OK" and "Rumford" that more easily confirms its former purpose.

One of the lesser-known suppliers of early baking powder bottles was the Sea Gull Specialty Company of Baltimore and New Orleans. Unlike Rumford and Davis, whose bottle bottoms were generally plain, Sea Gull Specialty embossed its name on the bottle's bottom and shoulder. Its primary production facility was in full swing in Baltimore in the early 1900s. These unique shards have at times been found by sea-glass collectors with merely the word "SEA" showing. Of course, those who have found them are quite fond of those items, but the company also produced another brand in tin cans with a bit less romantic title, "Parrot and Monkey Baking Powder."

Circle M – Cobalt Blue

The bottoms of glass bottles commonly provide key features for estimating their age and can at times reveal the identity of the manufacturer. In general, bottle bottoms prior to the 1850s rarely had embossed numbers or text; by the late 1800s, some crude numbers and text were used. Then in the first half of the 20th century, automatic bottle machines helped makers' marks become common on the base along with mold numbers. By the 1950s, textured edges and stippling patterns were added to help process bottles faster. While bottle lips can divulge a great deal about the general time period a glass vessel was created, it is a mold-made bottle bottom exhibiting a manufacturer's logo that helps to narrow down a date of origin. Most numbers on bottle bottoms refer to its mold cavity, except the numerals just to the right of a logo, such as the Owens-Illinois diamond that displays a date.

Cobalt-blue sea glass has long been a collector favorite. The circle M logo seen on this cobalt-blue shard is a good example of how to identify history in general. Several references can assist collectors when searching for bottle-maker marks. This circle-M belongs to the Maryland Glass Corporation.

The company was founded by Captain Isaac Emerson in 1907 to create bottles for his rapidly growing Bromo-Seltzer business. Emerson was an owner of several drug stores in Baltimore before he decided to trademark his unique Bromo-Seltzer product in 1889 and establish the Emerson Drug Company in 1890. He promoted his remedy as ideal for headaches, sleeplessness, and alcoholic excesses.

Emerson built Maryland Glass Corporation and hired Philip Heuisler to run the operation. Its first bottles from 1907 to 1916 have a lone "M" on the base without any circle. It was in 1916, when they began exclusive use of Owens' automatic bottle machines, that the circle M logo was created. They continued using cork closures until 1920, when they began molding bottles for screw-cap closures. Between 1907 and 1936, Maryland Glass was said to be the largest producer of cobalt-blue bottles in the world. They produced cobalt-blue bottles for Phillips, Noxzema, Vicks, Wyeth, Squibb, and more. Many of these were made into the 1960s. The circle-M logo was not frequently used on these bottles but remained on Bromo-Seltzer bottles until they stopped producing them in the mid- to late-1950s.

Handles and Stems

Some collectors find ring-like shards and have difficulty imagining their origin. The objects shown at right in amber glass and one shown in the center are typical molded jug handles from the 1940s to 1960s. They display mold lines on the rounded handle exterior. In 1939, Clorox launched their first half-gallon jug with a circular finger ring in amber glass and then followed it with millions in gallon sizes. Round rings, also known as loop handles, were regularly molded onto gallon jugs for cider, wine, vinegar, and chemicals during the 20th century.

In the center, a large handle was possibly once used to raise a pint-sized beer mug. The similar gray handle on the left could have been part of a leaded glass carafe or pitcher, a bit more formal than a common beer mug.

In front, the broken portion of an applied pitcher handle displays a unique opening similar to that of a Calla lily flower. And at the top, a similar shard in Kelly green is rarer since its handle was possibly for a juice or lemonade pitcher.

The use of handles to pour from large glass vessels is nothing new. Roman glass makers applied handles to many of the jugs and amphora vessels they produced.

Scroll Flasks

Pear-shaped pint, half-pint and quart flasks with two swirls meeting at the base became commonly known as "violin" or "scroll" flasks. Initially produced around 1830, their elaborate French scroll design was, at times, decorated with a six-pointed star in the center, alleged to recognize the Free Mason influence of that era. They were produced by several glass houses in New York, Pennsylvania, West Virginia, and Kentucky.

This extremely rare shard from Lake Michigan included a partially polished, iron pontil mark on its base, placing it roughly around 1850. Aqua was the most common color for scroll flasks, which were popular in the 1840s and '50s but not frequently produced after the mid-1860s. Thus, most scroll flasks will have pontil scars on their base.

One of the most comprehensive references on the diverse assortment of 19th-century flasks is George and Helen McKearin's *American Glass*. These bottles, along with many pictorial flasks, are popular with collectors as their ornate designs were prized possessions and few were tossed aside as waste in the years of peak use.

Bee Brand

In 1889, an innovative 25-year-old in Baltimore, Maryland started a company with three friends providing root beer and other flavoring extracts to the local community. Young Willoughby McCormick was a savvy marketer. He decided early on to call his product line the "Bee Brand" and, by 1895, had the "Clover" brand as well. The following year, he purchased a spice company that remains a global giant to this day. While there is limited information on why he selected the bee as his initial brand, one guess is a remote connection to his first name.

This shard, easily mistaken for a honey container, was found on one of the disappearing islands of the Chesapeake Bay. It displays a detailed embossing of McCormick's registered trademark bee surrounded by what appears to be a belt. That particular circular-belt design is similar to the logo used by Charles H. Phillips on his Milk of Magnesia bottles, introduced a few years earlier. Many of the Bee Brand bottles used for his extracts were clear glass, and several others are triangular shapes in cobalt blue—the latter possibly for some poisons. So, this amber shard is quite rare and likely dates from 1890 to 1920. Today, a more familiar "Mc" logo for McCormick is found on grocery shelves where vanilla extracts and assorted other seasonings await those wishing to add flavor to meals at home.

Stoppers

Traditional glass stoppers were popular on sauce and drug bottles in the late 1800s. Some had ground-glass shafts and others a layer of cork to create a secure seal. Rarer finds are pressed-glass stoppers developed when molds advanced at the turn of the 20th century. In this image, a cruet-style stopper appears to have a diamond or pineapple pattern while the head of a perfume stopper displays a floral motif. Both show a hint of lavender, while a typical sauce bottle stopper below it shows a more vibrant hue of purple. This color reveals their age as pre-1915, due to the presence of manganese within the glass, which gives them the lavender hue. On the right is a finial top once on the lid of a small sugar bowl or similar container. In the foreground is a rare, iron-stained, Wm. H Brown Brothers perfume stopper from their Baltimore perfumery, which began in the mid-1800s.

These items were found on the beaches of several remote Chesapeake Bay islands. The islanders were supplied by steamers in the late 1800s that brought goods from surrounding cities and then returned with fresh seafood and eggs from the island.

Turlington Patent Medicine

In the early 1700s, English medicine bottles were rather basic except for their paper labels boasting patents granted by the King of England. One of the earliest known embossed bottles exported to the U.S. from England was Robert Turlington's Balsam of Life. He was granted a patent by King George II in May of 1744 for his complex mixture of 27-named ingredients. Ten years later, he began producing a very unique, violin-shaped bottle to protect his equity from a growing crowd of counterfeiters. He boldly squeezed onto his small 2 1/2-inch bottle, "BY THE KINGS ROYAL PATENT GRANTED TO" on one side, and "ROBT TURLINGTON FOR HIS INVENTED BALSAM OF LIFE" on the other.

So this first-of-its-kind, embossed patent-medicine bottle became commonly used in colonial America for its implied abilities to cure kidney and bladder stones along with a host of other ailments.

In the early years, the Turlington bottles were imported into Williamsburg, Baltimore, and Philadelphia, then later into New England. The compact medicine became a popular tool of explorers and was one that was specifically requested by Lewis & Clark for use on their 1804 journey westward.

By 1824, the newly formed Philadelphia College of Pharmacy had published information on several popular English patent medicines, including a feature of Turlington's Balsam of Life. Some have speculated that Thomas W. Dyott took notice of this and began making some of his own concoctions before later establishing himself as one of Philadelphia's glass manufacturers.

Turlington's Balsam of Life had great success in the states from the mid-1700s to 1900, except during years when tariffs and other conflicts with the British prevented sales.

T.W. Dyott

Visit a bottle show and you will get the chance to see gorgeous vintage flasks from early American glass houses. One popular collectible is the original Thomas W. Dyott American Eagle Flask. This vibrant cobalt-blue shard is an uncommon color for a flask that was mostly produced in light blue. The "T.W." prefix is an easy detail to see along with the eagle claw, the lower tip of a shield and an arrow.

Dr. Thomas W. Dyott immigrated to Philadelphia around 1795 and later began working alongside druggists before soon starting to make his own nostrums. He reportedly gave himself the title of doctor to help sell his medical formulas faster. His assorted pictorial flasks were initially produced at the Philadelphia and Kensington Glass Works in the 1820s, which he acquired and renamed Dyottville Glass Works in 1833. It was established as a unique glass factory community with strict rules and some rewards like housing and education for those staying within the boundaries of decency. The concept failed during the depression of the late 1830s after Dyott, who had started his own bank that later collapsed, was imprisoned. By 1844, the glass factory restarted under a new owner, who continued production of thousands of flasks with the T.W.D. initials during the mid-1800s.

17th Century Wine Bottom

Bottle collectors familiar with colonial wine bottles are accustomed to seeing 18th century, Dutch-onion-style wine bottles with wide bases that typically measure at least 5 to 6 inches across. These normally curve rather sharply upward from the base at what is called the heel and are built with sturdy, thick glass in this lower section. On this unique bottle bottom, the same area of the heel is far thinner, the glass core and surface extremely crude, and its gradual slope upward from a small 4-inch base indicates this was not a sturdy wine bottle crafted for overseas transport. Its heel rises up at a more gradual angle and is constructed of very thin glass. These features suggest it is most likely a 17th-century English wine bottle used for serving wine tableside. A small shard alone would have been much harder to date. The extreme bubbling in the glass itself suggests hand-blown materials from the top of an inadequately cured batch of pre-1750s glass. However, a draw from deeper into the pot of molten glass might have yielded glass with far less bubbling, making it difficult to date.

"I HAVE SPENT MANY HOURS ON THE BEACH COLLECTING SEA GLASS...WHO USED IT? WAS IT A MEDICINE BOTTLE? A BIT OF A SHIP'S LANTERN? IS THAT BUBBLED PIECE OF GLASS WITH THE CHARRED BITS INSIDE IT FROM A FIRE?"

— ANITA SHREVE

UNCOMMON GOODS

Vanishing History

On an early June weekend visit to Smith Island in Maryland, my wife and I were introduced to artifact hunter and 12th-generation resident Tim Marshall. The island sits precariously in the heart of the Chesapeake Bay just inches above sea level, one of the lone survivors among neighboring atolls that have succumbed to rising water levels. To fully enjoy this picturesque island located a brief 40-minute boat ride from Crisfield, Maryland, visitors will need to plan ahead. When we called to set up a beachcombing tour, Tim confided that he and especially his girlfriend, Tricia Richards, were great fans of sea glass. They had received our *Pure Sea Glass* book long ago, a present from the Chesapeake's most gifted nature writer and steward, Tom Horton.

Not long after arriving at our Inn, we were welcomed by Tim and Tricia who had come to set up a time for our tour. Tricia was beaming and clearly excited to show me a special shard. It was a marvelous Colonial wine bottle seal, the best I've ever seen found as beached glass. The gem formerly adorned the shoulder of a wine bottle belonging to J. Lewis in 1730. Tim's friend, Danny Hill, picked it up on a beach near Crisfield. I was eager to learn more about its original owner once getting home. After seeing that treasure and hearing Tim's promise to find "a lot of old stuff," we were ready to jump into Tim's skiff as soon as possible.

Discovering historic shards is always possible on the Chesapeake Bay. There ships have plied brackish waters and spilled cargo since the 1600s, and some a bit more during rum running years. The abundance of black glass is second only to the historic glass relics found on Bermuda. Collecting these remnants before rising waters withdraw them back to the deep is a race against time.

In the early 1900s, several of the islands near Smith were vacated. On them, residents routinely buried trash in pits that many decades later washed into the Bay and up onto the shorelines. By 1920, abandoned islands were left to the elements. Even tattered graveyards have been overcome by tides and waves over the years. Tim and other native islanders shared stories of helping to return or move caskets to higher ground before they began drifting away. The beachcombing experience was surreal, with every step and every reach one was sure to pick up material remains at least 100 years old. It was informal beach archaeology at its finest, without the meticulous excavating and record keeping. Marshy beaches almost devoid of sand in many places yielded artifacts from middens deftly exhumed by Mother Nature alone. Tim's favorites are the Native American Indian's projectile points—like arrowheads—that are many thousands of years old. The rest of us were focused on items a bit more contemporary.

While not all the glass shards were as buffed and worn as one might expect from rougher sandy shores north of this region, many did have adequate wear. The color assortment found during our visit was exceedingly diverse due to the many tableware items once broken and discarded from the missing homes, where now only small

aggregates of brick foundations remain.

Over the next several pages, there will be an assortment of historical shards and objects from the islands in this region. Their stories greatly reflect the rewards of researching the origins of these special finds.

Smith Island Treasure

A RELATIVE'S RING

One day while walking on the shore of Smith Island, Tim found what appeared to be a very large ring. It was so large he initially questioned whether it could have possibly fit the size of anyone's finger. He noted it had eleven notches on the inside of the band and, on a hunch, went to speak to a relative on the island to get some feedback. What he heard made perfect sense. His great aunt's husband was a waterman, who went crabbing, fishing, and oystering for a living like almost everyone on that island during the 1900s. That life has a way of toughening the hands, and the man was not only as strong as an ox but apparently as big as one too. He raised nine children. The relative noted that there would have been 11, but a set of twins died at childbirth, thus two notches cut into the ring closely side by side were for the lost twins. Tim had his mystery solved. This ring of a distant relative, Grant Parks, was possibly lost while working or when his grave succumbed to the bay.

HOLLAND ISLAND

Due north of Smith Island is an uninhabited island with merely grave markers hidden in salt grass, the oldest of which dates to 1817. What was once five-square miles of homeland for over 350 people in 1900, became victim to erosion from rising water levels and storms, especially during 1914 and 1918. Those who had funds moved their homes to the Maryland mainland. By 1922, Holland Island was uninhabited, and only 120 acres of mostly marsh still remain. Just days after my visit to this ghostly marshland with Tim, I was back in Chestertown, two hours north, and met a woman whose ancestors once lived on Holland Island. She recalled as a little girl visiting there and watching her family replace coffins of relatives that were becoming exhumed by the elements. When I called Tim a few days later to share her story, he asked me her name. When I hesitated for just a moment, he asked, "Was she a Parks?" She sure was. His next guess would have been Price, both the earliest two families to settle on Holland Island. A review of historical records reports William A. Parks as an owner of the island. This pendant, found by Tim, was said to be some form of club medallion for local inhabitants. William A. Parks was born on Holland Island in 1801 and died in 1884, while his presumed son by the same name was born in 1833 and died in 1915. The specific family member the medallion belonged to and how it was lost to the waters of the Chesapeake remain unknown.

1730 Wine Bottle Seal

The harvest year for wine stored within a bottle adorned with its buyer's blob seal leaves no mystery for determining its date of origin. Another challenge is discovering who might have been enjoying its contents. One easy mistake is thinking that the consumer's first name started with an "I" rather than a "J." In those early years of the 18th century, the capital "I" with a line dissecting its center represented the letter "J." This type of text on a shoulder seal of a glass wine bottle during that period was common to wealthy plantation owners and merchants. Not many colonists had the level of wealth to receive wine from across the ocean with their name emblazoned on the bottle's side. For this glass shard found on the lower Chesapeake Bay, it was helpful to use the informative web site of Maryland's Jefferson-Patterson Park for identification of colonial artifacts. It confirmed this type of seal would have been for someone with the name J. Lewis.

An immediate search for 1730 plantation owners named John Lewis provided a direct hit. There appeared to be no others in the region with his background and status at that time. Colonel John Lewis IV owned a large plantation in Gloucester, Virginia and was a merchant as well. He lived from 1692 to 1754. Lewis owned several merchant ships that surely would have transferred goods around the Chesapeake Bay. His plantation estate, Warner Hall, remains in Gloucester today where it is used for weddings and special events.

John's younger brother was Robert Lewis, grandfather of the famed American explorer Meriwether Lewis. In addition to this historic connection, John's son Fielding Lewis married Betty Washington, younger sister of our first president, George Washington. It was also noted that the Lewis merchant ships assisted our troops during the American Revolutionary War. The shard, found on the shores near Crisfield, Maryland, was 54 nautical miles from Gloucester. During that time in history, the Chesapeake Bay was the equivalent of several major highways today. Transportation by water was far more efficient in colonial times than by land. However, goods shipped via the Bay were also targeted by opportunistic pirates, hiding among the islands of the Eastern Shore.

Buttons

Prior to the 19th century, hand-crafted buttons were significant signs of social status. The wearer's class and level of wealth were literally displayed on their sleeves with gold, ivory, gemstone, and even embroidered buttons. In some cases, buttons would be sewn onto different clothing on a daily basis since they were such highly valued adornments. Lower classes had limited access to durable sleeve buttons, which usually outlasted clothing and were transferred from one shirt to another. It would be rare to find a person of modest social status with more than one set. Up to the 1820s, primarily men wore buttons. One exception, of course, is the Amish community, who generally has avoided buttons, considering them a sign of vanity.

The black-glass button industry became highly active virtually overnight when fashion setter, England's Queen Victoria, began mourning her husband Albert's death in 1861. Her black jewelry and pearl-shaped buttons were first made out of jet, a fossilized coal found in England and Spain. Because of the high demand and expense of the lightweight jet, black glass was used as a replacement. The Industrial Revolution was in full swing, so in the late 1800s, black-glass buttons were ubiquitous fashion. However, by 1920, black-glass buttons had virtually gone out of style as lighter colors predominated.

A number of the Victorian-era, black-glass buttons were molded to create reliefs of plants and animals, or to depict pictorials and fabric patterns. There are thousands of designs used in the manufacture of black-glass buttons, but most can be dated between 1860 and 1920.

Fulgurites

The most fragile form of glass found on beaches and in dunes is a source not made by man. The coarse, root-like veins of ash, only rarely found on beaches, are called fulgurites for the Latin word fulgur meaning lightning. Some also call these lightning stones or petrified lightning. They are created when lightning strikes sand, which easily exceeds the 3200 degrees Fahrenheit (1800°C) needed to melt sand.

While their normally gray exterior appears like burnt petrified roots, their inner core can exhibit a smooth glassy tube or an interior similar to dark foamy glass, almost like bone. In areas such as south Florida, fulgurites can be more white or tan due to the sun-bleached coral sands in that region. Further north, fulgurites are often in darker, charcoal-ash tones such as the samples shown here from the dunes and beaches of Nags Head, North Carolina. Most range in size from 1/2 to 2 inches in diameter and can be found in lengths of 2 to 3 feet, but some have been found to be even longer.

If a collector believes they have come upon a fulgurite, they should carefully remove sand from around it and extract it very gently to keep it intact.

Radio-Strain Insulator

Most sea glass comes from superfluous broken bottles, while various forms of broken-glass tableware are a distant second in volume. A third, but less likely source of sea glass, is electrical insulators that served the general power and communications industries. Many collectors are familiar with glass insulators shaped like beehives and mounted on telegraph poles in the 19th century and telephone poles during the 20th century.

If a collector finds a unique item that clearly is not from a bottle or tableware, consulting an electrician can be helpful for identification and historical information. One good example is this "radio-strain insulator," which was often used in pairs or as a series to separate antennas or wires from contacting a tower or other nearby hardware. This particular insulator was popular during the 1930s and 1940s when HAM radio operators were widespread.

The vast majority of radio-strain insulators are clear glass, but there are a few light blue and lavender-colored ones. They usually measure about 3 to 4 inches in length. Several were also created in porcelain and offered in a few more diverse colors.

Art Glass

There are very few places on earth where shards of genuine art glass can be found tumbling amongst the pebbles and wrack at water's edge. Unlike bottles and tableware, artisan-crafted glass is rarely discarded. It is carefully handled and often passed down as a family heirloom. As a result, collectors who regularly find shards of art glass have done so in close proximity to an art-glass studio or factory.

Many could guess that the island of Murano in Italy, which is famous for its Venetian glass, is a good region for finding art-glass shards. Fewer know of a distant shore along the northeast coast of the United Kingdom, which also yields exquisite pieces near an old glass factory. Closer to home is a perilous beach near Davenport, California that has provided some of the most exquisite art-glass pieces anywhere. Each of these places has produced marvelous assortments of multi-colored shards, far more elaborate than two-toned shards of layered glass or pieces fused in a rogue seaside campfire.

Credit for the American Studio Glass Movement goes back to the late 1950s and is given to glass artist and educator Harvey Littleton. He organized the first glass blowing seminar at the Toledo Art Museum in the early 1960s, and the industry has since flourished. One of his early students was contemporary glass icon Dale Chihuly.

The unique sea-worn piece of art glass shown here was found near Davenport, California over 30 years after it was swept away from the nearby Lundberg Studio. A swollen creek behind the studio removed some scrap trimmings of glass left behind the workshop. The eye-shaped piece was apparently snipped off the bottom of a hot vase while being rolled during the shaping process. The distinctive daisy pattern is the result of white stripes that ran up the outer wall of the vase. This exemplary shard epitomizes the phrase, "one man's trash is another man's treasure."

Orphan Colors

Glass is a surprising material that continuously amazes and educates the collector. Within several years of gathering sea glass and studying bottles, one can easily spot a nontraditional glass color. There are only a few hues that really do not match any in the pallet of about 25 customary colors used in mass-produced bottles. Indeed there are some odd colors of tableware and especially unique colors of art glass, but when finding shards of sea glass from bottles in truly unfamiliar colors, we simply nickname them "orphans." After years of separating shards by color onto trays, we can quickly discern which ones truly do not fit in with the rest.

A few colors may have been purposefully created; however, many were likely production misfits. Odd colors could be produced by the purge of one batch for another or a simple formulation mistake when a small dose of a metal oxide was just enough to taint a short run. In some cases, the same oxidation process that creates familiar sun-colored lavender pieces affects glass differently when other metals are present in excess. A good example is gray glass from old sun-baked, leaded-glass objects. These can display a rare blue-gray tone if copper is also present in the glass.

Shown in this picture are several orphan shards we set aside over the years. The most unique is the one that transitions from off-white, to light blue, to a deep cobalt blue that is almost black. Some bottle collectors have nicknamed this color "blue-black." In most cases, sea-glass collectors who find these conclude they are black glass since very little blue is showing. Once looked at more carefully, an odd blue is evident and, when backlit, there's a big surprise. Bright light shows the core glass is actually an unexpected olive green. Near the shard is a more traditional olive-green type of black glass with just some light surface bluing. Since the bluing on these blue-black shards encompasses all the surrounding edges, the color is clearly not from an intentional surface treatment. Thus, one can deduce the color is from the oxidation of metal ions in the glass, such as cobalt or copper used in forming the blue, and tin or zinc in contributing the white. Meanwhile, the common olive-green tone within shows the dominance of iron in the

batch. In nearly every case, these show bubbling in the core, confirming these are likely colonial bottle shards.

In front of the blue-black piece is an unusual peacock-blue shard while farther back are extremely dark cobalt blues, much darker than normal cobalt blue. One shows the ribs from a possible poison bottle. Also, in the foreground, are unusually light-colored cornflower blues. Opposite them in back are unique periwinkle colors. The lone green pieces are a deep-teal tone—a lip shard from a late 19th-century pharmacy bottle and thinner shards possibly from its wall.

Serious bottle collectors don't get excited about Bromo-Seltzer bottles. However, this one is a fine example of orphan glass since its deep indigo-blue color looks nearly black in regular light. The hue of the bottle is quite different from the company's common cobalt blue; this one is almost midnight blue.

Wired Glass

On occasion, sea-glass collectors find shards of frosted clear glass with wire embedded within its core. Some find this perplexing, but those who attended schools or visit municipal buildings built in the 1950s and '60s are familiar with wired glass. Designed to prevent shattering in extreme heat, wired glass was often placed in fire doors.

First patented in 1895 by Edward Walsh of St. Louis, it was initially mass produced in England by Pilkington Glass in 1898. Wire was simply fed off a roller into molten glass. In later processes, it was sandwiched between sheets of hot glass.

Wired glass lost favor with builders in the 1970s when the material was found to have less impact resistance than some other safety-glass forms with glazed surfaces. New versions of wired glass with advanced glazes are strong and compliant with safety codes but still have not regained popularity.

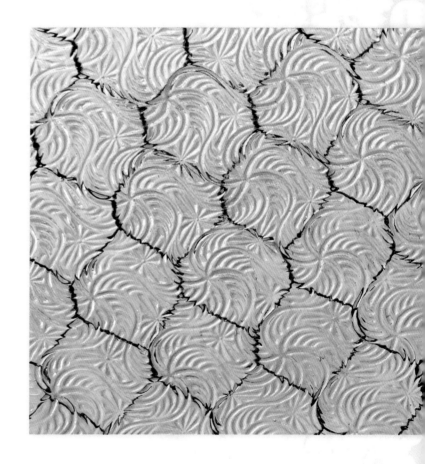

Clay Pigeons

On occasion, collectors have found opaque black shards that appear to have a ceramic or carbon core. No light passes through them since they are constructed with coal tar and calcium carbonate. These are fragments of clay pigeons used for skeet shooting. At times, a small amount of orange, white, or yellow glaze appears to be on the black shard, and possibly a strange pattern is embossed.

The object shown here is from a popular brand once owned by Winchester known as the White AA Flyer. It is still being produced today with coal tar, which displays a charcoal-black core. However, it is being replaced by gypsum-based materials, because the coal tar version contains hydrocarbons, which are not ideal for the environment or animals. Since the clay pigeon looks far more like a flying saucer than a bird, one may wonder where the name came from, as well as the command "pull" when a shooter is ready. In the early 1800s, Europeans went to great expense hosting hunting weekends on grand estates. But not everyone could afford such luxuries, and practicing before the hunt was a challenge. As competitions and prizes grew, birds such as pigeons and starlings were placed in boxes called traps, creating a new spectator sport. The shooter would yell "pull" to an associate, signaling him to pull a long cord that opened the box some 30 yards away. The bird would burst up and out of the trap, and soon a sport called trap shooting was popularized on both continents.

In America, trap shooting was growing, but by the late 1860s, glass balls stuffed with feathers were being substituted for live birds. These "target balls" were also being used in Wild West shows, as well as for competitions. Finally, in the late 1880s, the first clay disks were introduced in the U.S. and were made firm enough to be launched, yet fragile enough to be broken. Though much skeet shooting is done inland, a fair number of people enjoy shooting at sporting clay disks next to open waters, where broken remnants are later found by beachcombers.

Glass Trade Beads

I t is extremely rare to find a glass trade bead along the shoreline. The few collectors who do find these may mistake them for a more recent bauble, when they are actually holding an extraordinary piece of American history. Glass trade beads marked the arrival of Europeans to North America. It has been reported Columbus brought a number of these shiny little gems with him on his first trip to the New World. Explorers arriving on either coast of America knew the importance of this glass currency. They were known to have been exchanged with Native American Indians for land, furs, and provisions by the English, French, and Spanish.

Heavy concentrations of glass trade beads have been excavated from hundreds of Native American Indian sites along the Eastern U.S. and in parts of the Pacific Northwest. During the 17th and 18th centuries, possibly a thousand different types of glass beads were exchanged. Tumbled, round, or oval necklace beads in opaque black, blue, green, and burgundy were abundant, as well as some turquoise and white beads. Most of these colonial glass beads originated in Europe and were made by a process called "wire-wound" or "mandrel-wound" methods. This involved winding a molten thread of glass around a metal mandrel until a preferred diameter was achieved.

Note that the sky-blue bead in the center of the image is most likely made by the Dutch and was abundantly traded before and after 1600. This sought-after glass bead became relatively common, and sources note archeologists often find this color in infant Indian graves.

The glass trade beads shown in this image were found on the islands of the Chesapeake Bay in Maryland. The black beads, both round and oblong, are said to be from the mid-1600s. The blue and citron beads are from the 1700s, but the small white bead with pinstripes in the foreground is a Venetian trade bead possibly from the 1500s. All of the glass beads shown, with the exception of the small red one, were brought by settlers from across the ocean specifically to trade with the Indians for a variety of goods. Some Native Americans then adorned themselves with strings of beads—symbols of status.

Native Americans valued shell and stone beads long before and after the European settlers arrived in North America. Unlike glass trade beads, "wampum" were strands of shell beads, traditionally white or purple, created from clam and whelk shells, and were often strung together or woven into belts in patterns of significance. Read from right to left, they told stories of tribal history and agreements, and indicated the status of an individual, particularly that a person holding them was speaking truthfully. Finding wampum or glass beads would be a rare delight.

"ON SUCH A FULL
SEA ARE WE NOW
AFLOAT. AND
WE MUST TAKE
THE CURRENT
WHEN IT SERVES,
OR LOSE OUR
VENTURES."

— WILLIAM SHAKESPEARE

AWAKENINGS

What will the next wave bring ashore? Rising tides already conceal generations of glass artifacts more rapidly every decade. The echoes of our past are slowly dissolving into grains of sand or becoming lost to our sea floor.

Between 1860 and 1920, glass vessels mass produced for use by the general public were created across the spectrum of colors. The bottles displayed extraordinary style, but the art and originality of bottle design was virtually dismissed by the 1920s, when automated bottle machines replaced traditional hand-blown processes. The demand for greater output at less cost forced glass-production machinery into factories everywhere, and batch colors were soon consolidated into massive volumes of clear, green, and brown containers. A few exceptions in the first half of the 20th century included Coca-Cola's sea-foam green, medicinal cobalt blues, and the soft blue Mason jars.

Within 10 years after describing sea glass as one of nature's vanishing gems on the cover of *Pure Sea Glass*, dozens of collectors routinely mentioned seeing significant declines in sea glass. The popularity of collecting shards reduced supplies at some beaches so much that passionate collectors are now discouraged. While sea glass dwindles on local beaches, we are left to wonder what will become of this cherished collectible in coming years.

Many shorelines in parts of the Northeast are private, making it a challenge for some to enjoy the solace of a good beach walk, even off-season. Before our beaches are lost to the sea, it is a shame that they only be available to a limited few. Serious collectors from New England now travel abroad to coastal communities where they find more ample amounts of sea glass in vast colors.

It is ironic that the State of California restricts access to Glass Beach in the town of Fort Bragg, when the already diminutive shards that blanket its shore will continue to erode into microscopic pebbles. This was likely due to selfish collectors who scooped up buckets of sand and sea glass rather than looked patiently for a few meaningful pieces. A beach replenishment plan may one day be as vital to the future of that beach and community as it has been elsewhere. In the end, clean accessible beaches serve future generations just fine.

Holding on to History

Individuals who embrace history understand the value of studying the actions, thoughts, and objects created by those who lived before us. The accomplishments and gaffes of our predecessors can often inspire us to achieve more as we attempt to improve our world.

When a library, historical building, or any edifice significant to our past is destroyed, it eliminates an opportunity for first-hand exploration of our ancestral history. Often citizens will come forward to rescue structures from demolition, but some irreplaceable relics, manmade and natural, get tossed aside in the name of progress. Historic homes in coastal communities are now threatened by rising sea levels, as well as by being replaced by large, lucrative rental properties.

In old Nags Head, on the Outer Banks of North Carolina, is an important piece of history that could soon be lost to the fury of an Atlantic hurricane. Inside a weary 1920s bungalow patiently sits the most extraordinary and diverse collection of seaside relics ever amassed by a beachcomber. Known today as the Outer Banks Beachcomber Museum, this classic coastal cottage was once a local Nags Head grocery store and home to Nellie Myrtle Pridgen.

Nellie was a woman with one primary passion since the 1920s; she walked the beaches almost daily in search of treasure—not gold or silver—but virtually any items lost to the sea. Her gatherings from the shore are a time capsule of goods from the first half of our 20th century. Nellie spent the majority of her life methodically accumulating and researching over 50 years of American history, along with a few objects that predated her by several hundred years. Most of the collection is neatly archived in boxes or cases, on shelves, or in piles. This is not a hoarder's mess. Nellie was well read and understood history quite well, but the collection seems to have outgrown the modest cottage. Glass bottles and sea glass make up a noteworthy part of the menagerie. It includes exquisite shells like a rare Argonaut, tin soldiers and other toys, as well as a plethora of fulgurites left behind by lightning strikes in the sand. One remarkable find is the top section of a stoneware jug, featuring a bearded man's face, a rare piece of German Bellarmine vessel likely from the 1600s.

During World War II, Nellie watched the beach transform as forlorn items such as canteens, cans of rations, and even bodies began to wash ashore. But as the war ended, she felt invaded by a new and unexpected source—tourists. Tormented by the sight of chronic development surrounding her, she used trips to the beach as a time to escape. Like an encroaching tide on a child's sand castle, she had no means to hold it back. Soon she could no longer walk the beach, finally falling ill, and passing away in the summer of 1992.

In October of 2004, Nellie's daughter and son-in-law, Carmen and Billy Gray, ventured by train to the first ever sea-glass festival in Gloucester, Massachusetts. Enlisting the help of her close friends, Dorothy Hope and Chaz Winkler, they managed to bring up a portion of Nellie's collection to share her life-long treasures. Years later, Carmen passed away allowing Dorothy and Chaz to continue hosting intermittent museum tours for years. Unfortunately, development near the house left limited space for parking, so the museum is not allowed to remain open to the public. Dorothy and Chaz are trying to find ways to protect or move the building. Without resources to move the cottage away from the sea or from the encroaching calls for development, the most extraordinary beachcombing collection in history may soon be lost forever. Like sea glass, this building on our National Register of Historic Places, needs to be gently lifted and carried to a new home.

"SHE HAD NO IDOLS, EXCEPT THE OCEAN."

— CARMEN GRAY (speaking of her mother, Nellie Myrtle Pridgen)

AUTHOR'S NOTES

The core spirit of some sea-glass collectors has been altered a bit during this new century. Prior to the year 2000, there were very few artists creating sea-glass jewelry or other crafts with sea glass. They were an obscure minority in the art community and had very little exposure beyond local craft fairs and gift shops.

The advent of internet selling and sea-glass festivals raised awareness of the value of sea glass as a desirable adornment and quasi-organic art. Bits of seasoned glass were soon being swept from beaches by more than passive hobbyists; collectors with commercial interests needed sea glass to fill orders. In some cases, artists were bidding against others to purchase sea glass from online sellers or began hiring collectors to acquire shards. Ultimately, the competition between the tidelines almost became contentious.

Those who once stored their sea glass in containers as decorations and mementos of trips to the shore were hoping to cash in. A few even used shifty methods to mimic sea glass, but most collectors can easily spot the satiny and evenly pitted surface of artificial sea glass. As supplies of any highly valued object diminish, it is common that some will look for alternatives.

Karma finds a way to reward those with honest goals and discipline others with selfish intentions.

Rising water levels continue to cover up beaches once rich in sea glass, adding to the fevered competition for shards. Yet there is a positive side to the overzealous collecting of sea glass—one of environmental stewardship. The individuals who have used sea glass as an element in their craft have contributed to cleaner beaches. The value of that contribution is actually rather extraordinary.

In 2011, the World Bank estimated that if our American Coastal Shoreline Counties, including those along the Great Lakes, were considered an individual country, their Global Gross Domestic Product (GDP) would place third behind the total United States' GDP and China's GDP. The economic impact of clean, accessible, and desirable shorelines on local tax revenues makes coastal tourism one of our nation's greatest resources.

But we will all miss finding sea glass. Long ago, an acquaintance from a local family shared that when her beloved father passed away, a friend gave her a single piece of beautiful sea glass. She commented that it still remains as one of her most prized possessions.

At a Rhode Island memorial service for a young woman lost at sea during a sailboat race, mourners were encouraged to bring sea glass to place on the beach. A close friend of ours took his wife's sea-glass collection and returned it to the Atlantic on the one-year anniversary of her passing.

The tales of healing through collecting sea glass are just part of the story. There are also many uplifting accounts of family connections to sea glass. At one event, a woman noted that over 30 years ago, her mother had coined the phrase, "I had a red sea-glass day today." They both still use this expression when calling each other with great news. In Dewey Beach, Delaware, a man purchasing our first sea-glass book mentioned that he brought an engagement ring along for a walk on the beach and decided that if he found a piece of blue glass, it would be his sign to propose. He then added, now several kids later, "Guess what I found that day?"

The beach lures us to witness its infinite energy, constant motion, and change. We listen to its music for advice and solace. Each day is different. While we cannot control the waves, the shore presents to us only what we need for that moment, demanding anything more will surely leave us with less.

"IT IS A CURIOUS SITUATION THAT THE SEA, FROM WHICH LIFE FIRST AROSE, SHOULD NOW BE THREATENED BY THE ACTIVITIES OF ONE FORM OF THAT LIFE. BUT THE SEA, THOUGH CHANGED IN A SINISTER WAY, WILL CONTINUE TO EXIST; THE THREAT IS RATHER TO LIFE ITSELF."

— RACHEL CARSON

When Richard LaMotte and I were signing *Pure Sea Glass* books 11 years ago, it quickly became clear to me that the passion for these transformed bits of glass was profound and widespread. As I have photographed these treasures, I have witnessed over and over again the preciousness of sea glass to their collectors—richer than anything money could buy and valued for distinctly personal reasons. Richard's books represent this spirit.

I had been aware of sea glass. From the time I was a small child, I had always loved that place where the land meets the sea, but for some reason, sea glass was not plentiful on the beaches I knew. I came in by the back door when Richard invited me to photograph his first book. As I have touched, studied, and photographed prized collections over the years, I have come to know sea glass intimately.

All the images in this book are made with sunlight, sky light, or cloud light. Though the glass was photographed in studio settings, my desire was to be true to the feeling of the natural light of the beach. When I am working, I am always aware that the objects in front of me have been transformed. In a sense, sea glass is transformed again when a photographer focuses on it in a particular way, changes its scale, or captures some fleeting moment of vitality.

The physical richness of these forms and their luminous qualities are enough to make them enticing, but my experience is that some aspects of these gifts from the sea are invisible and incalculable. How does one photograph echoes of others' prior lives, memories of a day, or thoughts of a life's journey? Can a photograph convey what cannot be seen? I have an affinity for photographing with my camera only inches from my subjects, as though I am convinced that if I get close enough, maybe, just maybe, I might see inside and touch the miracle, touch the spirit within these things.

Thank you, Richard and Nancy LaMotte, for the opportunity to know sea glass so well and for the honor to be included in this thoughtful and insightful book.

ACKNOWLEDGEMENTS

Photographer: Celia Pearson

Editor: Sally LaMotte Crane

Design: Sara Birkemeier and George Scott, 8 Dot Graphics

Layout, editing and research: Nancy LaMotte, Sea Glass Publishing, L.L.C.

SEA GLASS COLLECTIONS:

Cover: Tim Marshall and Trisha Richards, Smith Island, Maryland, cover, pages 146, 147, 159, 160, 164, 167, 168-169, 173, 174, 188

Kirk Nelson, from the collection of The New Bedford Museum of Glass (NBMOG.org), Massachusetts, pages 8, 16, 17 and 23

Louise and Ben Rogers, Rogers Gallery, Mattapoisett, Massachusetts, pages 10-11, 62, 78, 92, 95, 202

Richard and Nancy LaMotte, Chesapeake Bay, Maryland

Susanna Swapana Hinnawi, Italy, pages 26-27, 35, 58-59 and 199

Annette Dashiell, Beaver Island, Michigan, page 156

The Beachcomber Museum, Nags Head, North Carolina, pages 178, 192 and 195

Mary Beth Beuke and Lindsey Furber, Salish Sea, Washington, page 47

Stu and Emily Jacobs Chesapeake Bay, page 81

HEALED BY THE SEA – STORIES:

Barbara Belton, "Corolla Cure"

Sue Jostrom, "A Fragile Heart"

Cindy Mathis, "Two Blue"

Stephen Fried, "Shard Inheritance"

Wendy Andrews, "Lost and Found"

Karen Welch, "Symbols in the Sand"

Louise Rogers, "Soul Searching"

Dave Sharrett, "Look Toward the Surf"

TREASURES BY REGION:

Danielle Perreault, The Sea Glass Center, Coastal Southern Maine

Louise and Ben Rogers, Rogers Gallery, Mattapoisett, Massachusetts

Holly L'Hommedieu, HL Sea & Beach Glass Jewelry, Long Island, New York

Stu and Emily Jacobs, Chesapeake Bay, Western Shore, Maryland

Richard and Nancy LaMotte, Chesapeake Bay,
Eastern Shore, Maryland

Brenda Hall, His Shells by Brenda, Outer Banks,
North Carolina

A.J. and Kimberly Koontz, Vero Beach, Florida

Jody Diehl, Beach Treasures (treasurebeaches.com),
Galveston, Texas

Lori Lambert, Capistrano Beach, California

Jayne Hawley, Monterey Bay, California

Krista Hammond, Santa Cruz Sea Glass, California

Mary Beth Beuke and Lindsey Furber,
westcoastseaglass.com, Salish Sea, Washington

Annette Dashiell, Beaver Island, Michigan

Terri and Jennifer Reed, Relish, Lake Erie, Pennsylvania

OTHER SEA GLASS CONTRIBUTORS:

Tim Marshall and Trisha Richards, Smith Island,
Maryland

Virgil Hibbs, Chesapeake Bay, Maryland

Dorothy Hope and Chaz Winkler, Outer Banks,
North Carolina

Ashle Cooper, South Carolina

Al Guy, Cambria, California

BOTTLE AND GLASS CONTRIBUTORS:

Bill Simms, Salisbury, Maryland

Olde Good Things Inc., Scranton, Pennsylvania

POETRY, COURTESY OF (IN ORDER OF APPEARANCE):

"Sea Glass for Margaret" by John Smith, Frenchtown,
New Jersey

"Cobalt Blue" by Bryan Cook, Ontario Canada,
©2013 Bryan Cook

"At The Leprosarium" by Eve Rifka, from the book
Outcasts: The Penikese Island Leper Hospital 1905-1921,
Little Pear Press ©2010.

"Rebirth of Sea Glass" by Marabeth Grogan, in Simply
from the Sea ©2009 Marabeth Grogan

"Beach Glass" by Richard Cambridge, Cambridge,
Massachusetts

"Sea Glass for Mimi" by Donald Werner,
©2015 Donald Werner

TECHNICAL CONTRIBUTORS:

Mark Newsome

Tim Marshall

Charles Sheppard

"SEA GLASS
IS BECOMING
MORE SCARCE
WITH EVERY
PASSING DAY."

— RICHARD LAMOTTE
FROM *PURE SEA GLASS*